£2

Reader's Digest Needlecraft Guides

APPLIQUÉ, PATCHWORK & QUILTING

Reader's Digest Needlecraft Guides

APPLIQUÉ, PATCHWORK & QUILTING

Detailed techniques and over 80 inspirational designs

Published by The Reader's Digest Association Limited
LONDON • NEW YORK • SYDNEY • CAPETOWN • MONTREAL

READER'S DIGEST NEEDLECRAFT GUIDE: APPLIQUÉ, PATCHWORK & QUILTING
First published 1995
Copyright © Text and Illustrations 1995, 1981

The material in this book first appeared in
READER'S DIGEST COMPLETE GUIDE TO NEEDLEWORK
First edition Copyright © 1981
Reprinted 1991
The Reader's Digest Association Limited,
Berkeley Square House, Berkeley Square, London W1X 6AB

Copyright © 1981 Reader's Digest Association Far East Limited
Philippines Copyright 1981 Reader's Digest Association Far East Ltd

Printed in Italy

ISBN 0 2764 2180 9

CONTRIBUTORS

The publishers would like to thank the following people for major contributions to this book.

Consultant editor Eirian Short

Editorial contributors and designers
Louise Amble   Peggy Bendel   Sherry De Leon   Rosemary Drysdale   Katherine Enzmann   Phoebe Fox   Zuelia Ann Hurt
Barbara H. Jacksier   Joyce D. Lee   Susanna E. Lewis   Claudia Librett   Victoria Mileti   Edna Adam Walker
Monna Weinman   Joanne Whitwell

Technical assistance
Elspeth Arnold   Lesley Arnold   Betty Beeby   Linda Blyer   Barbara Dawson   Janet Eaton   Charlotte Feng-Veshi
Sheila Gore   Jane Iles   Diana Keay   Elizabeth Kerr   Arlene Mintzer   Carole Nolan   Erwin Rowland
Cathie Strunz   Valentina Watson   Joan Webb

Contributing artists
Roberta W. Frauwirth   Susan Frye   Pat Kemmish   John A. Lind Corp.   Marilyn MacGregor   Mary Ruth Roby   Jim Silks
Randall Lieu   Ray Skibinski   Lynn E. Yost

Contributing photographers
J. D. Barnell   Bruton Photography   Joel Elkins   Ken Korsh   Russ McCann/Conrad-Dell-McCrann, Inc.   Michael A. Vaccaro

Research assistance
Aero Needles (Abel Morrall)   Appletons Bros Ltd   C. J. Bates & Son   Emile Bernat & Sons Co.   Bernina Sewing Machines
Boye Needle Company   Brunswick Worsted Mills Inc.   J. & P. Coats   Cowling & Wilcox   Craftsman's Mark
The D.M.C. Corporation   Embroiderers' Guild   Frederick J. Fawcett Inc.   T. Forsell & Son   Harrods Ltd
Harry M. Fraser Company   Hayfield Textiles   Hosiery Machine Co.   Kreinik Mfg Co.   Lowe & Carr   H. Milward & Sons
Newey Goodman   Paternayan Bros Inc.   Paton & Baldwins   Phildar International   Pingouin   Reynolds Yarn Inc.
Royal School of Needlework   Singer Company (UK) Ltd   Sirdar   Talon/Donahue Sales Div. of Textron   Joan Toggitt Ltd
Twilleys of Stamford   Vilene   Whitecroft Scovill   Wm. E. Wright Co.

Cover
Photography by Paul Biddle   Craftwork supplied by Sue Simmons

Appliqué

Wall hanging 'Landscape with Mountain' © Madge Huntington 1976

Appliqué basics

Tools and materials

Appliqué work is basically a sewing craft, and so it calls for much the same tools and materials. **Fabrics** are of course essential, but not necessarily in great quantities; scraps and pieces are usually adequate for a small project. Easiest to handle are smooth natural fabrics in a light to medium weight. Be sure that all the fabrics used are of the same type if they are to be laundered. Try to avoid loosely woven or extremely bulky fabrics; they can be very difficult to manage. If, despite this limitation, you still want to use a particular loose weave, back it with iron-on interfacing (see p. 13). Before using any fabrics, press out all wrinkles and creases.

To stitch an appliqué in place, use an all-purpose (size 50) sewing **thread**. For additional decorative stitching, you can use stranded cotton or pearl cotton. Sharps are a type of medium-length **needle** excellent for hand stitching. They come in different sizes to accommodate different fabric weights. Other needle types, such as crewel and chenille, have larger eyes, permitting thicker threads to be used.

Another essential tool in appliqué work is a sharp pair of **scissors**. Ideally, you should have two pairs, medium-size dressmaker's shears for general cutting, and small, pointed embroidery scissors for close trimming.

Other useful sewing aids include fine **dressmaker's pins** for holding appliqué in place, and a dressmaker's **marking pencil** or hard lead pencil for marking fabrics. **Thimbles** are handy if you are accustomed to using them. **Frames** and **hoops** are optional and should be used only if they will make your work easier. **Heavy tracing paper** and **coloured stiff paper** are helpful for copying or cutting out designs.

As an alternative to stitching appliqué down, you can use **fusible webs,** which you can buy in packets. See p. 11 for the fusing technique.

Design ideas

Inspiration for appliqué designs can be found in many sources, among them colouring books, greeting cards and everyday objects. Traditionally the designs are quite primitive and childlike, rather than works of art. A typically simple design can consist of a central motif cut from a single piece, or perhaps made up of two or more pieces. A composition, in contrast, is somewhat more difficult and consists of many motifs that together form a complete picture. If you are a beginner, start with designs consisting of one or a few large pieces.

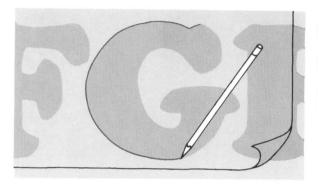

The monogram letter is a typical one-piece design. It is being *traced*, which is the simplest method for obtaining a design. If traced drawing is not the desired size, enlarge or reduce it to your liking by methods described in the Embroidery chapter.

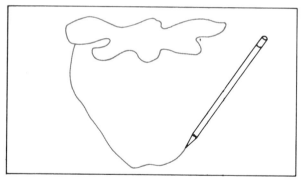

The single strawberry exemplifies a simple design of two main pieces. It is being *drawn freehand*, which is another way to obtain a design. Freehand designs can come from your imagination or from a model. Drawings need not be precise; in fact, simplified lines and details work best.

This sheep design is a composition created by first *cutting free shapes* of stiff paper, then arranging them to form a pastoral scene.

Making templates

If you have cut out some shapes from stiff paper to arrive at a design, or if you have cut out pattern pieces from a book or pattern, those pieces become the actual templates. If, however, you have traced or drawn a design, you will have to make templates for each separate shape in the design (see below). When appliqué is employed in patchwork, a single design may be duplicated many times over, which means the patterns are used again and again. In such instances, it is wise to re-cut the patterns from very heavy paper so that the templates will not become too worn to use.

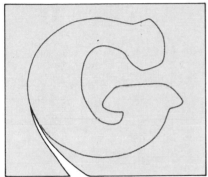

To make a template from a tracing or drawing, simply cut along the drawn outline of the appliqué piece. If the template is to be used many times, re-cut it from heavy paper or thin card.

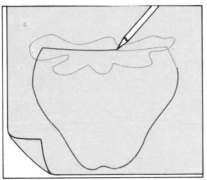

If your design consists of two or more pieces, re-trace each piece separately. Straighten out edges that will be covered by another piece instead of trying to fit the two pieces together.

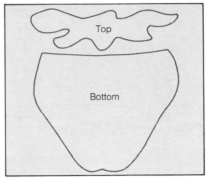

Cut out each separate piece along the drawn outlines. To avoid any errors when cutting the actual appliqué, mark the right side of each pattern piece with an identifying word or symbol.

Transferring designs

Before transferring a design, cut background fabric, which may be a patchwork block or even a garment section, to desired size. In order to centre the design accurately, mark vertical and horizontal centre lines through the background piece. The centre lines are especially helpful in patchwork because they enable you to position the appliqué in exactly the same spot for each of the blocks involved. A single appliqué may be placed in position on the centre lines by eye only, but for greater accuracy position marking is recommended.

To determine centre lines, fold and crease background fabric in half, then in quarters. Open fabric out, and for a firm guideline, tack along vertical and horizontal creases.

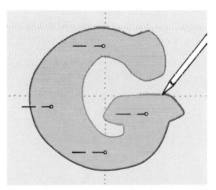

To transfer your design, position template, right side up, on background fabric and pin in place. Trace around template, using either a sharp dressmaker's pencil or a hard lead pencil.

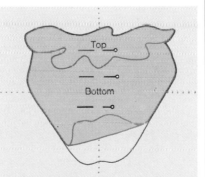

If a design has two or more pieces, carefully assemble all pieces in position, then pin them to the background fabric. Trace around design formed by the combined templates.

Other design possibilities

Paper cut-outs are another good source of designs. This kind of snowflake is often seen in traditional Hawaiian quilts. Because of its intricacies, hand stitching is advised and it is usually accompanied by echo quilting (see p. 14).

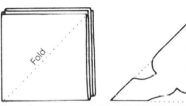

To make a paper cut-out, fold square sheet of paper in quarters, then in half diagonally. Cut out pieces through all thicknesses, then open out.

Using a fabric print is a quick and easy way to obtain an appliqué design. Simply cut 1 cm to 2 cm outside design silhouette and machine-stitch appliqué print to background fabric (see p. 10).

7

Appliqué basics

Cutting appliqué

The first step, if you will be cutting much appliqué, is to assemble your fabric scraps and decide which ones will be used for each piece. Try to achieve a balance of colours as well as a balance of printed and plain areas. If the fabrics you have selected have a dominant print or weave, consider carefully how you want that print or weave placed on each appliqué piece. For example, if a fabric is striped, it can be cut so that the stripes run vertically or horizontally. Always cut appliqué to follow the grain of the background fabric. This will give the best results.

Another consideration is the compatibility of the appliqué fabric and the background fabric in terms of care. Generally speaking, if the appliquéd article will not be laundered, almost any combination of fabrics is acceptable. If it will be laundered, be sure that all of the fabrics you plan to combine can take the same kind of washing and drying.

To cut out an appliqué, follow the step-by-step instructions given on the right. Note that staystitching is recommended to make it easier to turn edges under. If an appliqué has curves or corners, the seam allowances need to be clipped or notched to facilitate turning.

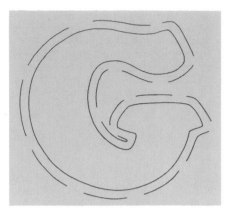

1. Pin template to right side of fabric. Trace around pattern with dressmaker's pencil. Remove template. Mark a 3 mm to 5 mm seam allowance outside the drawn seamline. Use the wider seam allowance on fabrics that are loosely woven.

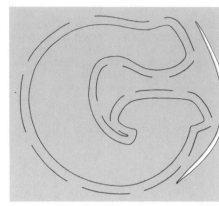

2. Cut appliqué outside marked lines so that an ample fabric width is left. This wider margin will make it easier for you to staystitch in the next step.

3. To facilitate turning under of edges, staystitch just outside inner marked seamline. Set sewing machine to sew short stitches.

4. Trim margin by cutting appliqué on outer marked lines as shown. Clip seam allowances around curves and corners so edges can be properly turned (see below).

Handling curves and corners

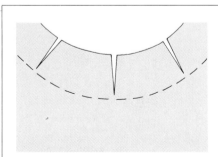

Along inner curves, clip seam allowance to staystitching to aid turning. Space the clips closer together along deeper curves.

Along outer curves, notch out pieces along seam allowances to keep bulky pleats from forming when edges are turned under.

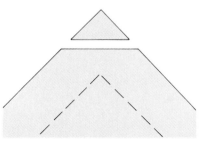

At outside corners, blunt seam allowance as shown to help reduce bulk in the point when the edges are mitred (see opposite page).

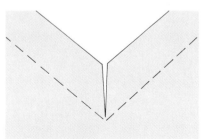

At inside corners, make a single clip into the point of the corner (up to staystitching) so that the edges can be turned under.

Securing appliqué by hand

An appliqué can be hand-stitched in place by either of the two methods shown below. The first method, though somewhat more time-consuming, is recommended for beginners. It calls for an additional tacking step that holds the turned-under seam allowance in position, making it less awkward to secure the appliqué to the background. The second method omits the initial tacking of edges; instead the appliqué is pinned in place, and the edges turned and stitched.

To secure the appliqué, a fine slipstitch is recommended; it holds the appliqué securely and is almost invisible when carefully worked. Oversewing stitches, though not invisible, should be used in small areas that tend to fray; these little straight stitches can keep the short fabric threads from popping out (see below). Embroidery stitches such as running stitch and cross stitch can also be used to fasten down an appliqué. Remember that these are decorative stitches, meant to be seen; they will become part of the design (see p. 14).

The use of a hoop or frame is optional. Some find stitching easier without one, while others find it a necessity.

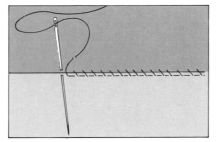

Paris stitch. Work from right to left. Bring needle out of appliqué just above the edge. Insert needle below and make a horizontal stitch to left. Replace needle in hole it came out of and make a diagonal stitch up and to the left.

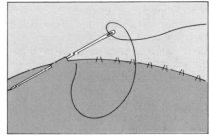

Slipstitch. Work from right to left. Bring needle up through folded edge of appliqué. Pick up thread opposite on background fabric then slip needle through folded edge for 3 mm. Bring needle out and pull thread tight.

Methods of sewing appliqué

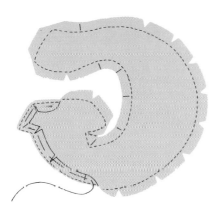

Method 1. Along marked seamline of appliqué, fold and finger-press seam allowance to wrong side; tack folded edge as you finger-press. Keep staystitching within the seam allowance width.

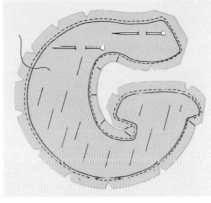

Method 2. Pin cut appliqué to the background (edges are not yet turned under). If needed, hold appliqué in place with vertical tacking. Be sure that stitches do not extend into seam allowance; edges must still be turned under.

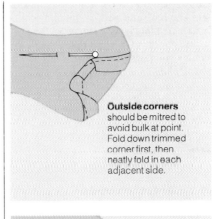

Outside corners should be mitred to avoid bulk at point. Fold down trimmed corner first, then neatly fold in each adjacent side.

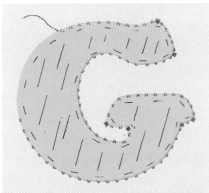

Pin appliqué to background and, if necessary, hold in place with vertical tacking stitches. Secure appliqué with a fine slipstitch along folded edges. Remove all tacking.

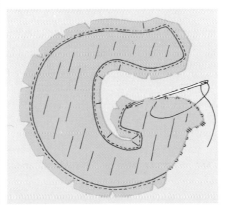

Using point of needle to tuck seam allowance under, slipstitch turned edges in place. Be sure staystitching is turned in with seam allowance. Continue to turn and stitch in this way until appliqué is fully secured. Remove all tacking.

To avoid fraying at corners and deep curves, oversew with small stitches at these points instead of slipstitches.

Appliqué basics

Securing appliqué by machine

The sewing machine is used extensively in appliqué work today because it makes it possible to complete a project in less than half the time it would take to do a similar project by hand. A decision to stitch an appliqué by machine instead of by hand can depend upon several factors. First, if the fabrics you are working with are relatively substantial rather than fine and delicate, they will be easier to handle with the sewing machine. Another consideration is the ultimate use of the appliquéd article. If it is likely to get a great deal of wear (a child's dungarees, for example), a machine application is undoubtedly more practical.

There are basically two methods of machine appliqué. One is done entirely by means of straight stitching; the other, which is considerably faster, uses a combination of straight and zigzag.

Before starting, test and adjust the machine so its tension is balanced and the pressure is correct for the fabrics being used. For straight stitching set the machine to medium stitches. When using thin fabric, zigzag stitching is usually narrow, with a short stitch length.

Straight-stitch method

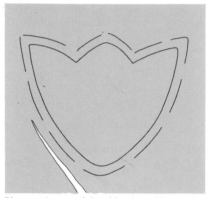

Pin template to right side of appliqué fabric. Trace around pattern and remove it. Mark 5 mm seam allowance outside marked line. Cut outside marked lines, leaving ample fabric width.

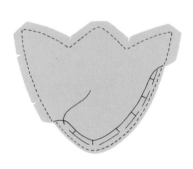

Staystitch just outside inner marked seamline. Trim excess margin by cutting on outer marked lines. Clip and notch curves and corners. Fold seam allowance to wrong side; tack in place.

Position and pin appliqué to right side of background fabric; if necessary, tack appliqué down with vertical tacking as shown to keep appliqué from shifting during stitching.

Set sewing machine to medium stitch length. Carefully stitch along folded edges of appliqué. Pull thread ends to wrong side and knot. Remove all tacking threads.

Zigzag method

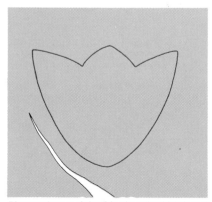

Pin template to right side of appliqué fabric and trace around it. Remove pattern. Cut out appliqué outside marked lines, leaving an ample seam allowance (approximately 1 cm to 2 cm wide).

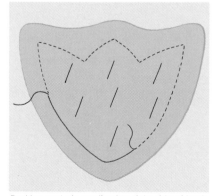

Position and pin appliqué to right side of background fabric; if necessary, tack appliqué down with vertical tacking as shown. Straight-stitch directly over the marked seamline.

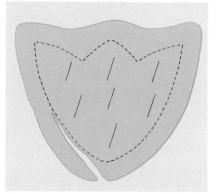

Using a sharp pair of pointed embroidery scissors, trim away seam allowance, cutting as close to stitching line as possible; be careful not to cut the stitches or the background fabric.

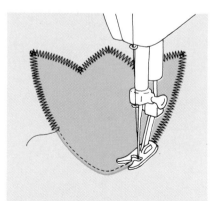

Select suitable width and length for zigzag and sew over raw edges and straight stitching. Pull thread ends to wrong side; knot. Remove tacking.

Zigzagging around corners and curves

Right-angle corners. Zigzag down one side of corner and stop at point shown by dot. For *outside* corner, position needle outside of point. For *inside* corner, position needle inside of point. Pivot and zigzag down other side of corner.

  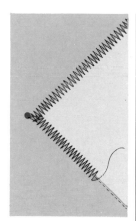

Wide-angle corners. Imagine a line running through centre of corner. Zigzag down one side of corner and stop when needle hits imaginary line at dot. For *outside* corner, position needle on dot outside of corner. For *inside* corner, position needle on dot inside of corner. Pivot and zigzag down the other side.

 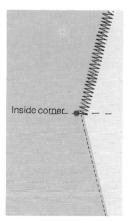 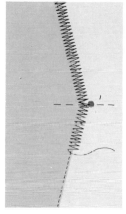 

Sharp-angle corners. Zigzag down one side of corner. Shortly before reaching point, start narrowing zigzag width. Continue stitching to just beyond corner (zigzag by then will be very narrow). Pivot and zigzag down the other side, gradually widening zigzag back to original width. Technique is the same for both outside and inside sharp corners.

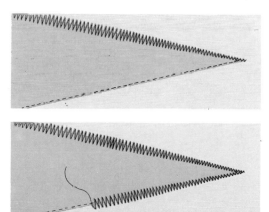

Tight curves. Zigzag down one side towards curve. To get around curve, stop and pivot work often, positioning needle on the narrower side of the curve each time work is turned. The technique is the same for both outside and inside curves.

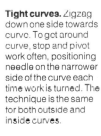 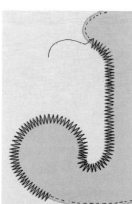

Securing by fusing

Appliqué can be secured with a fusing web, a bonding agent that holds two fabrics together when it is melted between them. Fusing works best on large appliqué pieces; alignment of appliqué and web becomes difficult with small or intricate shapes. Follow manufacturer's instructions carefully for a bond that will hold during normal cleaning.

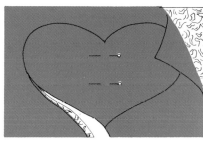

Pin fusing web to wrong side of fabric; treat two as one layer. Pin template to right side of fabric; trace around. Cut out appliqué on marked line.

Pin appliqué and web to right side of background; be sure they are perfectly aligned. Heat-fix appliqué by pressing between pins with tip of iron.

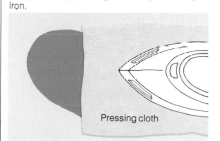

Pressing cloth

Remove pins. Place damp cloth over appliqué. Hold iron on cloth until area is dry. Lift iron and move to next area; do not slide iron.

11

Appliqué basics

Planning appliqué layering order

If the design of your appliqué is made up of two or more pieces, a certain amount of planning must be done to work out a numerical *order of layering*. This plan of action establishes the order in which the appliqué pieces will be laid down so that elements that should appear below others are properly positioned to do so.

This type of planning is especially important if the design consists of many pieces (see example, below right).

Use a drawing of your design as a map for your layering plan. Number each piece in the order in which it should be laid down. The elements that lie lowest are number 1, and subsequent layers building upwards are numbered 2, 3, and so on. When layering order is established, each piece is stitched down in numbered sequence. All the pieces numbered 1 are stitched first, then pieces numbered 2 and 3, until the design is completed. An exception can be made to sequential stitching if you are making several such appliqués. With this method, all pieces are pinned in layering order, then stitched at random. The result is not as neat as with sequential stitching, nor as secure, since hidden edges are not finished. But it is faster and, if the item is quilted, the incomplete stitching will not matter.

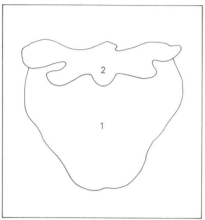

1. Make a layering plan on your drawn design by numbering each piece from lowest layer up. Following numbered plan, lay out actual appliqué pieces on marked background fabric as a check.

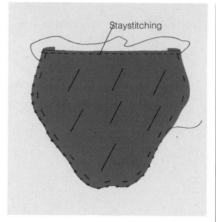

2. Remove all pieces except those numbered 1. Secure layer 1 in position, leaving unturned the edges that will be completely covered by another piece (top edge in the example above).

A layering plan is especially important in intricate compositions such as the sheep design shown here. As the numbering shows, six separate layers have been established in this design.

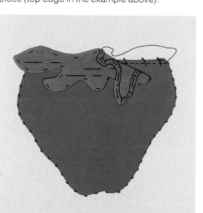

3. After the turned edges have been secured, use oversewing along the unturned edge of the appliqué as shown; this will prevent a bulky ridge showing through at the overlap.

4. Pin and stitch layer 2 in position, covering the raw edges of layer 1. If the design has more layers, continue layering and stitching in this way until the composition is completed.

In this illustration, layers 1 (cloud and mountain), 2 (meadow), and 3 (feet) have been appliquéd; layer 4 (bodies of sheep) is being pinned. Note how composition is being built from bottom layer up.

Using bias strips in appliqué

When a design calls for a thin, gently curved strip of fabric (for example, a stem), use a length of bias strip instead of cutting a thin, curved appliqué piece that can be difficult to manage. The bias strip has some stretch and can be shaped to the curve. Commercially packaged bias tapes are convenient, and are made in a range of colours.

To make your own bias strip, find the true bias by folding it diagonally so that a straight edge on horizontal grain is parallel to vertical grain (1). Press fabric on diagonal fold, open it out and use crease as a guide to mark parallel lines the desired width of the strip plus 1 cm for seam allowances (2).

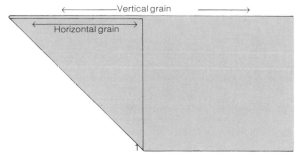

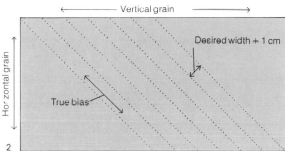

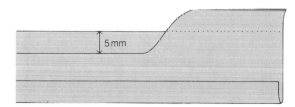

Cut bias strips along marked lines. Press under 5 mm seam allowance along both long edges of the cut bias strips.

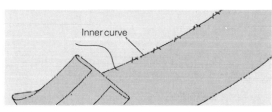

To secure, pin bias strip to background fabric, stretching it as necessary to conform to the desired curve. Secure the inner curve of the strip first.

Gently stretch outer edge of bias strip to shape to the curve; secure in place. Press bias strip after it is secured.

Interfacing an appliqué

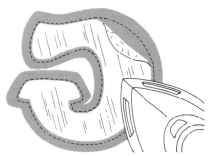

Appliqué fabrics that are limp or loosely woven usually need interfacing to give them stability and body for easier handling. Lightweight iron-on interfacings are usually the most convenient and can be bought by the metre. The wrong side of the interfacing is covered with a special bonding agent that will melt and adhere to another fabric when a hot iron is applied.

To interface appliqué, cut out appliqué as usual (see p. 8). Place template on *wrong* side of interfacing and trace. Cut out interfacing along marked line; do not leave any seam allowances.

Centre the interfacing over the appliqué so that wrong sides are touching, then press interfacing in place following the manufacturer's instructions. The appliqué is now interfaced and can be handled as you would a normal appliqué piece.

Stuffing an appliqué

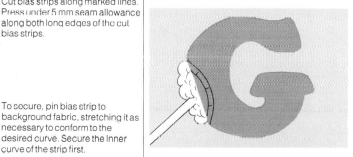

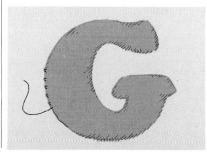

To add dimension to some appliqué designs, you can stuff the appliqué or parts of it with a soft wadding, thereby bringing the appliqué into relief. Either cotton or polyester wadding is suitable for this type of work.

To stuff an appliqué, first cut and secure it in place as described on pp.8–9; instead of completely fastening the appliqué down, leave a small opening in a strategic area, and carefully stuff wadding through opening with a blunt needle or stick. Distribute the stuffing equally, but do not overstuff; this might distort the appliqué.

When you have finished stuffing the appliqué, stitch the opening down. Manipulate stuffing in this area if it has become flattened.

Appliqué basics

Decorating appliqué

Decorating with embroidery or quilting can greatly enhance the overall look of any appliqué design. Even though you may not deliberately plan on any such embellishment, possibilities may occur to you after your appliqué is completed. There is a vast array of **embroidery** stitches to choose from; you can use them to work out original details or special effects, or simply as a decorative means of securing the appliqué in place.

Quilting is another decorative device that can add immeasurably to appliqué, particularly for patchwork appliqué.

Before quilting is begun, a layer of wadding and one of muslin are placed under the appliqué background and all three are tacked together. The simplest form of quilting is called *outline quilting* – a single row of running stitches sewn around the entire design, or parts of it, to emphasise its silhouette. Several quilting lines stitched concentrically following the outline are known as *echo quilting*. These can add a whole new dimension to a design. Quilting stitches can even be part of a composition (see sheep illustration, lower right).

Embroidered details add a touch of realism to the simple appliquéd strawberry.

Embroidered cluster of grapes gives originality and charm to the appliquéd block initial.

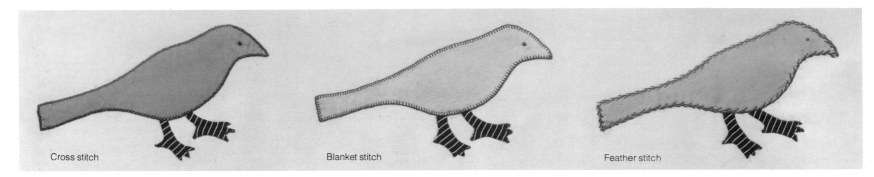

Cross stitch

Blanket stitch

Feather stitch

A different embroidery stitch is used to edge each of these appliquéd birds. The decorative stitches not only hold the appliqué in place, but also contribute colour and texture to the individual designs.

Outline quilting, stitched just outside motif, silhouettes and emphasises appliqué cut from fabric print.

Echo quilting radiates from an appliquéd motif. Technique is popular in Hawaiian quilts.

Quilting stitches are sometimes introduced as a part of the design itself. Here lines of quilting have been stitched to simulate falling rain.

Reverse appliqué

General introduction

Reverse appliqué, like surface appliqué, involves multiple fabric layers, but they are handled differently.

Reverse appliqué is known, in its traditional form, as **San Blas appliqué**, in honour of its best-known practitioners, the Cuna Indians from the San Blas Islands off the Panama coast. Even today, their colourful primitive designs decorate the front and back panels of the blouses, or *molas*, of the San Blas women. Their motifs are usually radiating, silhouetted shapes of people, plants and small creatures. These, plus slits that add strokes of colour, give this intriguing appliqué form its unique look.

Aspects of this traditional technique have been adapted to create a modern form of reverse appliqué that is known as **cut-through appliqué**. This technique can be successfully used with large, simple, bold designs like the sun design illustrated.

The basic difference between the traditional and modern forms of reverse appliqué is the order in which layers are cut and stitched, and the relative complexity of technique that this imposes. To produce the intricate channels of San Blas appliqué, you must work from the bottom layer up, cutting and stitching as each layer is added. Simpler cut-through designs require far less exacting techniques than those of the traditional method. For cut-through work, all fabric layers are tacked together at once, and shapes are cut out from the top layer down, producing larger to smaller 'shaped holes'. Special colour effects are made possible by variations on each technique; these are explained on the following pages.

Fabrics for either technique, ideally, should be tightly woven, lightweight, 100% cotton, and opaque. (Synthetic fabrics are too springy to turn under.) When you have chosen a pleasing combination of plain colours, find a matching thread for each fabric colour.

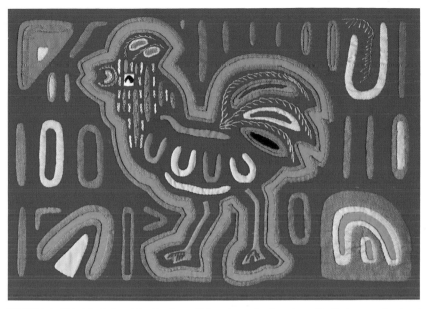

San Blas appliqué is distinguished by the radiating shapes and random slits. Surface appliqué and embroidery can also be used. This animal design was worked from the bottom layer up.

Cut-through appliqué is stencil-like in appearance. The fanciful sun design was systematically stitched and cut from the top layer down.

Reverse appliqué/San Blas

Basic technique

San Blas appliqué can be improvised, but to do this without losing the characteristic look, you must understand the basic technique, and the equal importance of the areas both *inside* and *outside* the drawn shape. When you work with only two layers of fabric, the drawn shape is cut from the top layer; at this point, depending on how the cutting was done, three different effects can occur (see variations on right). By interchanging these effects, you can get a variety of images, whether you use two layers, or decide to add a third. The total is rarely more than three, even in the most seemingly complex designs.

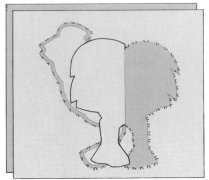

When a drawn shape is cut on the top layer, **the area inside can be removed,** and cut edges of outside area turned and stitched to bottom layer.

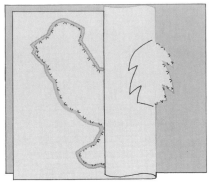

Or the area outside the drawn line can be removed. This time the cut edges of the inside area are turned and stitched to the bottom layer.

As a third alternative, **both inside and outside areas can be kept,** and cut edges on each side turned and stitched to create a channel.

Using two fabric layers

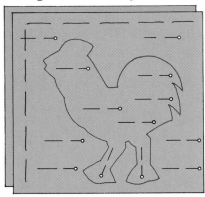

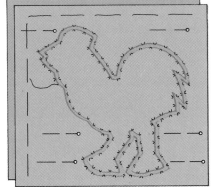

Using a total of only two fabric layers, you can still achieve the distinctive linear effect typical of San Blas appliqué.

1. Lay second fabric layer on first layer and tack them together around two edges. Draw or trace the main shape on to the top layer, and pin the two layers of fabric together inside and outside the drawn line.

2. Cut along the marked line, being careful not to cut layer below. Using point of needle, turn under the cut edges of the inside shape and slipstitch it to the layer below; clip curves. Cut and sew a small piece at a time for the best results.

3. Now turn and stitch the cut edge of the outside area the same way to produce the coloured channel that defines the shape. Remove pins.

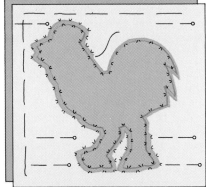

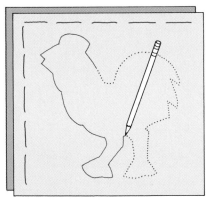

As a variation, a *third colour* can be added without adding a full third layer of fabric. This new colour can cover either the inside or outside areas of the drawn shape. In the example, the third colour covers the outside area.

1. Follow Steps 1 and 2 in instructions above. Remove tackings and take away parts of the top layer that are not stitched down.

2. Lay the third fabric over the first pair and tack fabrics together around two edges. With a sharp pencil, feel edges of main shape below and trace around it. Pin the layers of fabric together outside the traced line.

3. Cut along line of top layer only. Remove inside area to expose second colour below. Turn and stitch cut edges to bottom layer. Result is three colours, but only two full fabric layers.

Using three fabric layers

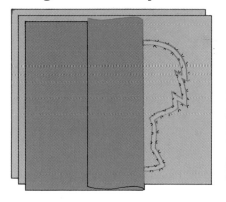
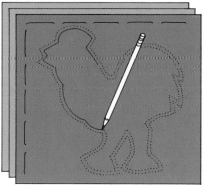

Using a total of three fabric layers, you can achieve more elaborate linear effects.
1. After working first two layers (see opposite page), place third fabric layer over them, and tack all three together around two edges.
2. Using a sharp pencil, feel edges of finished channel below and trace around it. Pin all three layers of fabric together inside and outside the drawn channel lines. Now you must decide which part of the layer will be cut away and which part will remain (see Basic technique). Example shown is just one way to handle this third layer.
3. Cut along the inner marked line first. Turn under cut edges of the inside shape and stitch to layer below. Cut along outer marked line; turn and stitch the cut edges, turning enough to expose a total of three different channels.

Using slits in San Blas designs

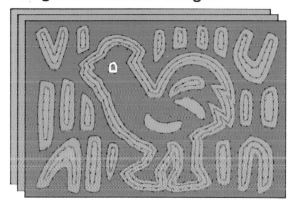

The series of elongated slits within the main motif and in the background is a typical feature of all San Blas appliqué. The slits are either *straight, angular* or *curved,* and are used at random according to the design's configuration. Slits can be worked on the second layer as well as the third.

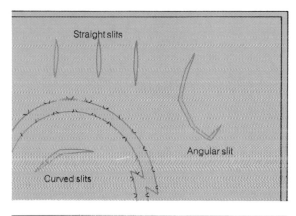

Straight slits

Curved slits

Angular slit

1. Draw desired slit lines on the uppermost fabric layer. Slits can be positioned in any direction. Cut on marked line through top layer only.

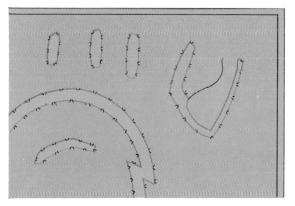

2. Using point of needle, turn cut edges under and stitch to the layer below, clipping as necessary to get around the curves and corners.

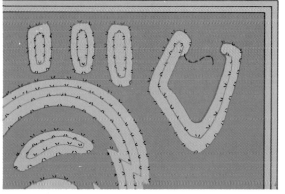

If third layer of fabric is added to piece already worked with slits, proceed first with the channelling of the main shape as described above. With a sharp pencil, feel edges of slits and trace around them. Cut along marked lines, then turn under and stitch cut edges to fabric layer below. An additional channel of colour will be revealed around the original slits as shown. New slits can be added to the top of the third layer as well.

Reverse appliqué/San Blas

Using coloured patches

Coloured fabric patches are another way of getting more colour into your San Blas piece without adding whole layers of fabric. This technique, like most of the San Blas methods, is intended to be improvised and can be introduced whenever you would like to add an extra colour. Merely tack fabric patches of the desired colours and sizes between any two layers of fabric; then cut away small shapes and slits to expose the additional patch colour below. In the examples shown, patches are applied to both the first and second layers. Select colours that will give you a strong contrast.

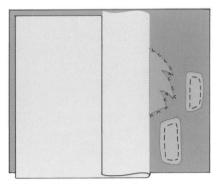

1. Cut and secure main motif (bottom left, p. 16). Position patches as desired; tack in place.

2. Lay next fabric layer over first layers and tack together around two edges.

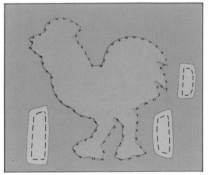

3. Complete the channelling of the main motif as described on p. 16.

4. Feel patched areas below; cut and stitch slits or shapes over them to reveal their colour.

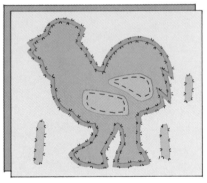

5. Position more patches over the top layer of fabric and tack around each.

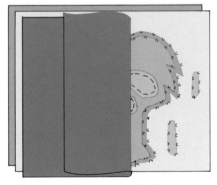

6. Lay another fabric layer over the first group and tack together around two edges.

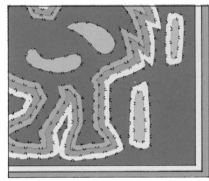

7. Complete channelling of main motif, then of the slits and smaller shapes over patched areas.

Using shaped patches

Another patch possibility in San Blas appliqué is a shaped patch. Its edges are meant to produce a predetermined contour, and are revealed to achieve that. This requires the patch to be cut to a definite shape and its edges finished neatly before the next layer is put down. Shaped patches, like standard patches, can be used between any two layers. A shaped patch along the edge of a major motif will change its overall silhouette and add interest to the colour (see example). The patch in the example is added to the first layer, with the main motif already stitched down (see p. 16).

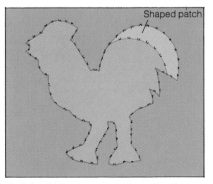

1. Cut patch to appropriate shape. Position over desired area; turn and stitch edges in place.

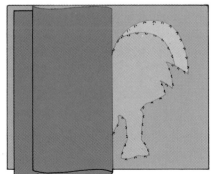

2. Lay next fabric layer over first layers and tack together around two edges.

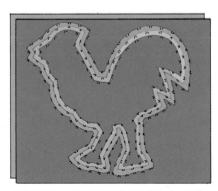

3. Trace around motif, and complete channelling as desired to reveal edges of shaped patch.

Reverse appliqué/Cut-through

General introduction

Cut-through appliqué is worked with all layers tacked together first, then shapes cut away to expose the layer below; five layers are the maximum number used.

The first shape that is cut from the uppermost layer must be large enough to accommodate each subsequent shape to be cut within it. Cut-through designs are usually free and bold, and have an almost sculptured look. Because of the bolder designs, this technique can also be done by machine (see next page).

Sometimes a layer can be exposed out of sequence by cutting through one or two layers above it. Additional coloured patches can also be added if desired.

Basic technique

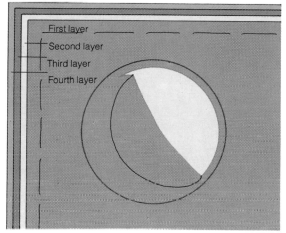

Cut desired number of layers to same size and stack them; tack together around outer edges. Trace or draw main shape (face) on top layer. Cut 3 mm inside marked line; do not cut layer below.

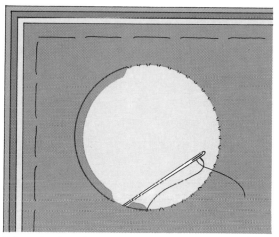

Using point of needle, turn under cut edge, clipping seam allowance as necessary to turn it under. Slipstitch turned edge to fabric layer below, letting a few stitches go through all layers.

Draw smaller parts of design that lie within the main shape. Decide which shape or shapes will expose third layer (in this instance, the mouth). Cut and stitch shape the same way as before.

Special cut-through techniques

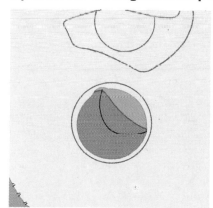

To miss a layer, cut shape (cheeks) from *two* top layers; cut brown one slightly deeper so edges lie under upper cream layer. Turn and stitch edges of upper layer to orange below.

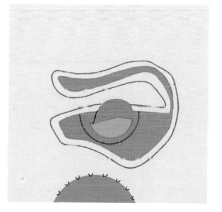

With this multiple layer procedure, you can work a detailed area so that two shapes touch one another (rather than one lying inside the other). First cut away the larger shape (eye unit)

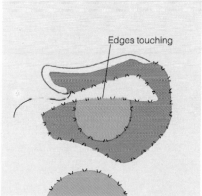

from top layer; do not secure edges yet. Draw and cut the smaller shape (eyeball) from newly exposed layer. Turn and stitch edges first of the smaller shape, then of the larger shape.

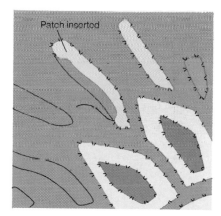

To add another colour, draw and cut shape (sun ray) from top layer. Cut a patch 5 mm larger than cut piece. Insert patch under upper layer, then turn and stitch cut edges to patch below.

19

Reverse appliqué/Cut-through

Basic machine technique

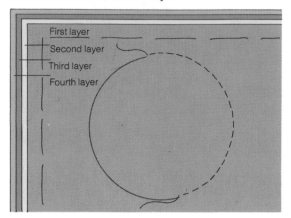

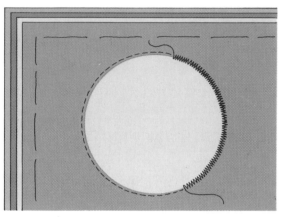

Cut desired number of layers to same size and stack; tack together around outer edges. Draw main shape (face) on top layer. Set short stitch length and straight-stitch on marked line.

Cut top layer just inside stitched line. Adjust sewing machine to suitable length and width of zigzag, then sew around cut shape to cover the raw edges and straight stitching.

Draw smaller parts of design that lie within the main shape. Decide which shape or shapes will expose third layer (in this case, the mouth). Stitch and cut as described for larger shape.

Special machine cut-through techniques

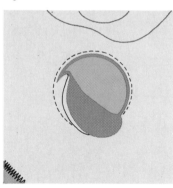

To miss a layer, straight-stitch around drawn shape. Cut away the shape (cheeks) from the two uppermost layers to expose the fourth layer below.

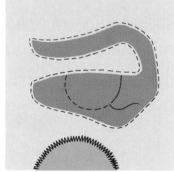

To work multiple layer procedure so two shapes touch, straight-stitch along larger marked shape (eye unit). Cut away shape just inside stitching line. Mark and straight-stitch the smaller shape (eyeball) on newly exposed layer.

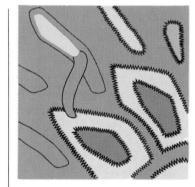

To add patch for extra colour, draw shape (sun ray) on top layer. Cut 3 mm inside the marked line. Cut a patch that is 5 mm larger than the cut-out piece.

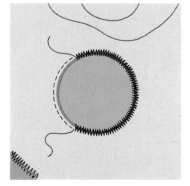

Zigzag over the cut shape to cover the raw edges and the straight stitching.

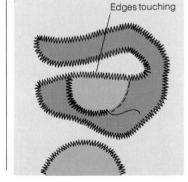

Cut away small shape inside stitching line. Zigzag over cut edges of both large and small shapes.

Insert patch under cut edges of upper layer. Straight-stitch on marked line. Trim seam allowance even closer to stitching line. Zigzag over the raw edges.

Patchwork

Quilt, 'Aurora' © 1976 Michael James

Patchwork basics

Types of patchwork

Patchwork is the joining of pieces of fabric to form a larger unit of fabric. The most interesting characteristic of any patchwork is the design that the joined fabric pieces produce. Some patchwork designs are simple and easy to analyse, others are so intricate that it is hard to tell how they were achieved.

The easiest type of patchwork to understand is the **one-shape** patchwork, in which all the pieces are the same shape and size. A one-shape patchwork can be worked in a single colour, but two or more colours, carefully arranged, pro-duce a more interesting design. An example of the one-shaped patchwork is the Shell design (first illustration below).

All other patchwork can be classified as **block-unit** patchwork, so called because the fabric pieces are first joined into a block that itself becomes the basic shape. There are two kinds of block units, pieced ('mosaic' patchwork where the patches are inlaid or joined edge to edge) and appliquéd (where the patches are sewn in layers to a background fab-ric). Most pieced block units consist of precisely shaped pieces that form a defi-nite design within a square; when sever-al such units are joined, a secondary overall design can be formed as in Sim-ple Star (below). Crazy patchwork is also a pieced block patchwork using ran-dom patches. An appliquéd block unit consists of an appliqué and the base fabric to which it is stitched. Appliqués tend to be stylised versions of realistic objects. For additional examples of patchwork designs, and instructions for producing geometric shapes, refer to pp. 24–29.

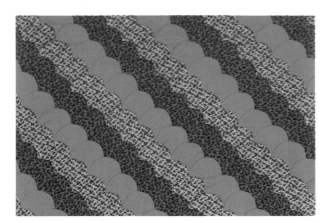
Shell design, a one-shape patchwork

Simple Star, a block patchwork of precisely shaped pieces

Crazy patchwork, a random-pieced block patchwork

Rose design, an appliquéd block patchwork

General considerations

Before any patchwork is started, two decisions need to be made simultaneously: the purpose of the patchwork, that is, whether it will be used for a skirt, a cushion, a quilt, etc., and the patchwork design. Certain considerations can influence both choices. One is your level of experience. If you are a beginner, it is best to start with a comparatively small project, and a simple design that does not have too many pieces. Also, you might find it easier to copy an existing design than to create one.

Another influential factor is the construction techniques advised for different types of patchwork. There are basically only two methods of construction, both explained briefly on the right. The first is recommended mainly for one-shape patchworks because the shapes associated with them are difficult to join accurately by any other sewing method. Hand sewing here is preferable to machine; it adapts better to the variations involved in preparing and joining the pieces (see pp. 46–48). The second method is used for block-unit patchwork; in this case, joining may be done either by hand or by machine. Shapes that can be joined with straight seams will be easier to sew than those requiring cornered or curved seams. For more details on sewing block-unit patchwork, see pp. 34–45.

Also to be considered are the size and number of pieces that will be needed to produce the finished patchwork. Both of these are determined in the course of charting the entire patchwork (p. 31). In general, the more pieces a design involves, the longer it will take to make the patchwork. It should not be assumed that a large finished size necessarily means a great many pieces. A single block of Simple Star (opposite page), for example, can be made quilt or cushion size. Regardless of its size, each block would take the same number of pieces; in this particular case, 17.

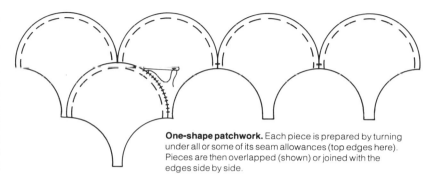

One-shape patchwork. Each piece is prepared by turning under all or some of its seam allowances (top edges here). Pieces are then overlapped (shown) or joined with the edges side by side.

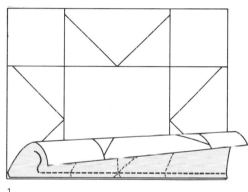

Block-unit patchwork. This type of patchwork can be sewn by hand or machine. First, the pieces are joined to form the individual block units (illustration 1). If it is a pieced block, the pieces are seamed to each other; for an appliquéd block, the appliqué is stitched to the base fabric. Next, the blocks are sewn together into strips of blocks (illustration 2). Finally, the strips are joined to complete the patchwork (illustration 3).

1

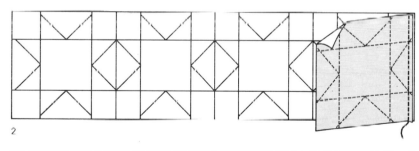

2

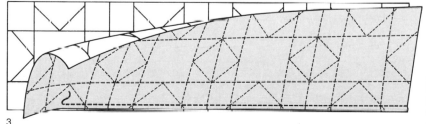

3

Fabrics and equipment

The fabrics for a patchwork should be compatible in weight, construction and care requirements. Similar weight and construction makes them easier to join and ensures that, when the fabrics are joined, one will not overpower and weaken the other. Medium-weight, evenly woven natural fabrics work best. When fabrics have common care requirements they can all be cleaned in one way, either laundering or dry cleaning, with no fear of some being ruined.

Before buying any fabrics, chart the entire patchwork (p. 31). A chart gives you a preview of the finished patchwork design, and it becomes the basis for experimenting with and deciding on suitable colour and print combinations. With a chart, you can also determine the exact size of each piece and then make templates (patterns) for cutting them out. Templates are also used to calculate how much of each fabric is needed to carry out the patchwork (p. 33). When you buy fabrics, try to find colours and prints that match or come close to those on the chart. If you are not sure how the fabric colours and prints will work together, buy a small amount of each and make a test patchwork. If you like the result, you can then buy the necessary quantities.

Certain drawing and sewing tools are needed. For designing and charting, you will need pencils, graph paper, a rubber, a ruler and colouring pens. A compass will help you to draw curves and circles; a protractor is used to divide a circle. Use heavy paper or thin card to make the templates. Scissors, pins, hand or machine sewing needles and thread will be needed for cutting and sewing. Thread should be either white or a colour that blends with the fabric colours. To mark fabric shapes and their seamlines, use a dressmaker's pencil. A white pencil is recommended for marking dark fabrics; a pink or blue pencil is best for marking light-coloured fabrics.

Patchwork basics

Designing with squares and diagonal lines

Of all the shapes used in patchwork, the most frequent is the **square**. It is possible to draw a very accurate square on graph paper, using its lines as guides.

During the designing of a pieced block, the square can be any size, but before templates are made it must be drawn to finished size (p. 32). In both design and template stages, the square is divided into smaller squares equal in size and number, across and up and down. These inner squares form the grid used to produce the shapes of the pieced design. The simplest division of a square is two squares across by two down, or a 2 × 2 grid, but other and finer divisions are possible (see below). The more squares in a grid, the greater the number and the variety of potential shapes. The pieced block designs on these two pages show the development from simple to complex patterns. To make it easier to 'see' the basic structure, the underlying grid of each has been emphasised in the drawings.

Some pieced block designs consist of just the grid squares, for example, the Chequerboard (1). In other designs, grid squares are grouped to form rectangles or larger squares; one such block design is Patience Corner (9).

Diagonal lines are introduced to form more intricate shapes. A diagonal may be drawn through a square or a rectangle; in either case, it is a straight line drawn from one corner to the diagonally opposite corner. When a diagonal line is drawn through a square, two half-square triangles are formed; when drawn through a rectangle, it produces two half-rectangle triangles. The triangles may be used as they are, or grouped with other triangles, squares, or rectangles to create shapes. Half-square triangles are the basis of the Windmill (2). Pairs of half-square triangles with their diagonal edges in opposing directions form the four larger triangles along the edges of the Simple Star (4). Pairs of half-square triangles with their diagonal lines parallel produce the rhomboid shapes that represent the 'scraps' in the Basket of Scraps (6). The centre piece of the Sally's Windmill block (14) results from joining two half-rectangle triangles to a grid square. The unusual shape in each corner of Crusader (15) is a grouping of three grid squares and two half-square triangles. Much of the effectiveness of pieced block designs hinges on the assignment of colours to shapes. For guidance in this, turn to p. 30.

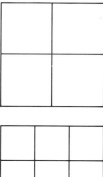

A grid is formed by dividing a square into smaller but equal squares. To do this, measure, then divide equally each side of the square; mark each dividing point. Draw grid by connecting sets of marks with straight lines from top to bottom, side to side. Shown left are a 2 × 2 grid (top) and a 3 × 3 grid (bottom). Right are a 4 × 4 grid (top) and a 5 × 5 grid (bottom).

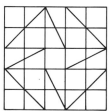

A diagonal line drawn between two diagonally opposite corners of a square or rectangle will form two triangles. The triangles can be used for the shapes of a design or grouped with other triangles, rectangles or squares. First illustration shows diagonals for Eight Point Star shapes (p. 222); the second, diagonals for shapes of Sally's Windmill (14, next page).

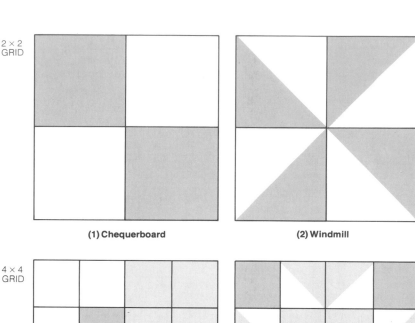

2 × 2 GRID

(1) Chequerboard   **(2) Windmill**

4 × 4 GRID

(3) Arthur's Garden   **(4) Simple Star**

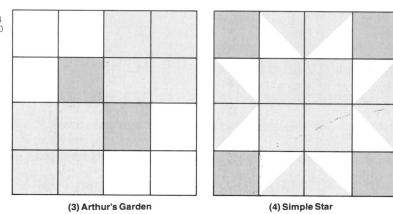

8 × 8 GRID

(5) Mixed Squares   **(6) Basket of Scraps**

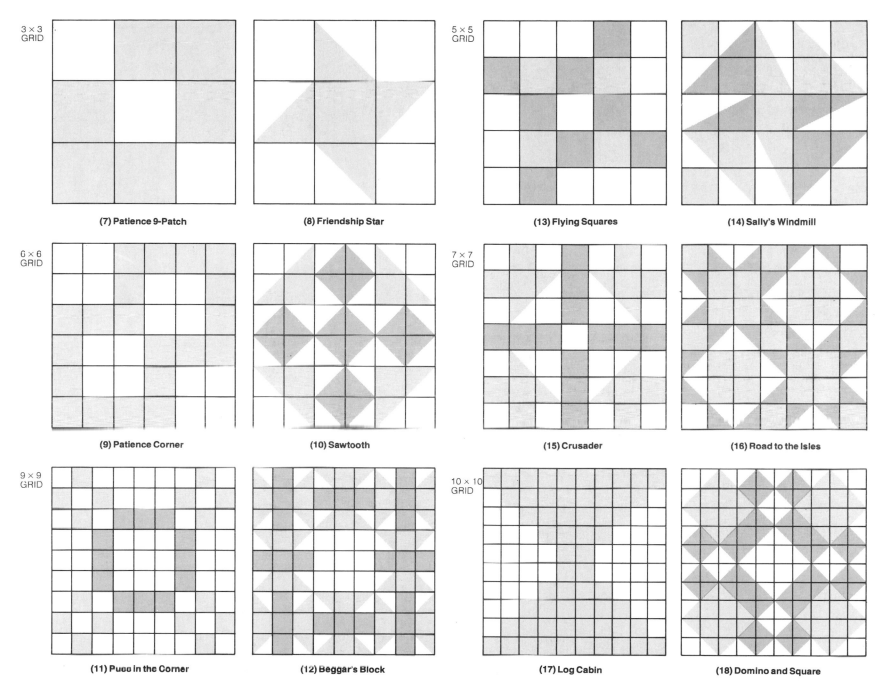

3 × 3
GRID

(7) Patience 9-Patch

(8) Friendship Star

5 × 5
GRID

(13) Flying Squares

(14) Sally's Windmill

6 × 6
GRID

(9) Patience Corner

(10) Sawtooth

7 × 7
GRID

(15) Crusader

(16) Road to the Isles

9 × 9
GRID

(11) Puss in the Corner

(12) Beggar's Block

10 × 10
GRID

(17) Log Cabin

(18) Domino and Square

Patchwork basics

Designing with circles and parts of circles

The use of circles and their parts to produce shapes is demonstrated by the patchwork designs on these pages. The techniques for forming the shapes accompany each design and are based on certain basic facts about circles.

A *circle* is a closed curve, of which all points are equidistant from a centre. Its perimeter is called the *circumference*. The distance from the centre of a circle to one edge is a *radius*, and equals half the circle's width. The *diameter* is the distance from edge to edge through the circle's centre (in effect, two radii); it equals the width of the circle. Any circle contains 360°.

A compass is used to draw a circle. Formation of a circle to a certain size is best accomplished by drawing it within a square. The size of the square and of the circle within it depend on the design

(see Dresden Plate; Grandmother's Flower Garden). Their common centre is located with vertical and horizontal lines that also act as diameters.

A portion of the circumference, called an *arc*, is also used to form shapes. A six-part division, with straight lines between division points, produces a hexagon (top of next page). An arc bounded by two radii creates a *sector*. Its shape depends on the length of the arc; that is determined by the degrees between radii. An arc equal to half a circumference and bounded by a diameter is a semicircle, containing 180° (see Shell). An arc equal to a quarter of a circumference and bounded by two radii at right-angles is a quarter-circle, containing 90° (see Shell; Drunkard's Path). To form a sector containing less than 90°, use a protractor (see Dresden Plate).

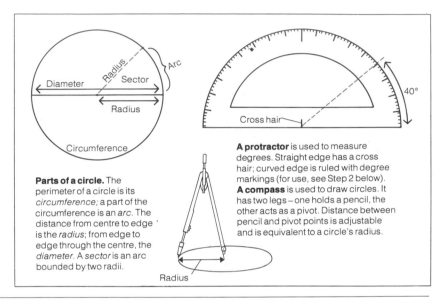

Parts of a circle. The perimeter of a circle is its *circumference*; a part of the circumference is an *arc*. The distance from centre to edge is the *radius*; from edge to edge through the centre, the *diameter*. A *sector* is an arc bounded by two radii.

A protractor is used to measure degrees. Straight edge has a cross hair; curved edge is ruled with degree markings (for use, see Step 2 below).
A compass is used to draw circles. It has two legs – one holds a pencil, the other acts as a pivot. Distance between pencil and pivot points is adjustable and is equivalent to a circle's radius.

Circles/Small sector

Dresden Plate

Concentric circles within a square supply the shapes for this appliquéd block design. The square determines the base block, also the large circle; from the large circle comes the **sector** for the wedge-shaped pieces. Small circle is the centre piece.

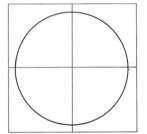

1. Draw a square (if you are making templates, draw it to finished size). Locate and mark the centre of each side. Connect marks on top and bottom edges with a vertical line, those on the sides with a horizontal line. The point where these lines intersect is the exact centre of the square. Place pivot point of compass on centre of square. Extend pencil leg out horizontally to a point close to the side of the square (if you are drawing a template to finished size, point is about 4 cm from side). Draw the circle.

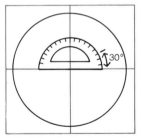

2. To determine the degrees in each wedge, first decide on number of wedges, then divide this number into 360 (circle contains 360°). Appliqué on left has 12 wedges; each wedge contains 30°. To form a sector with the desired number of degrees, proceed as follows: align straight edge of protractor along horizontal centre line; align its cross hair with vertical line. Find desired degree marking along curved edge of protractor and mark (30° in this case).

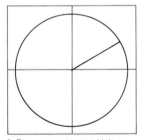

3. Remove protractor. Using a ruler, align the exact centre point of square and the angle marking. Hold ruler in place and draw a radius from the centre, through the angle measurement mark, to circumference of circle. Remove ruler. The horizontal centre line of the square serves as the second radius for the sector.

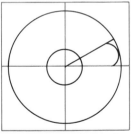

4. Working freehand, curve the outer edge of the sector as shown. Then place pivot point of compass on centre of square, and spread pencil leg enough to draw a small circle. Small circle is the finished shape for the centre piece of the appliqué. The sector, from its newly curved outer edge to the small circle, is the finished shape of each of the wedges in the appliqué. If making templates, only these two shapes need be drawn. If still in the design stage, roughly sketch in the other wedge shapes.

Circle/Small arcs

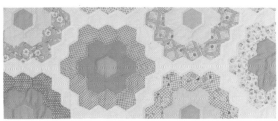

Grandmother's Flower Garden

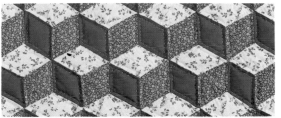

Baby Blocks

A circle divided into six arcs underlies a **hexagon,** the six-sided figure repeated in both patchworks on the left. *Grandmother's Flower Garden,* the first example, consists simply of small hexagons; the hexagons in *Baby Blocks* are large, and each is composed of three equal size **diamonds.** The first step in constructing a hexagon is to draw a square with sides equal to the height of the desired hexagon. The finished hexagon will be the same height as the square, but narrower. In general, the hexagons for Grandmother's Garden are 4 cm high by 3.5 cm wide, and the hexagons for Baby Blocks are 15 cm high by just over 13 cm wide.

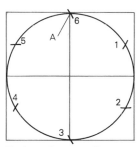

To draw a hexagon. Draw a square and find its centre (Step 1, facing page). Draw a circle same width as square. With compass at same setting, divide circumference into six equal parts by means of six arcs, 1 to 6. Draw first arc with pivot of compass at point A; draw each new arc with pivot at point where arc just drawn intersects circumference.

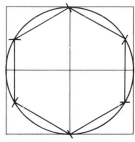

Then draw the six sides of the hexagon. For each side, line up two adjacent arc intersection points along the edge of a ruler and draw a straight line from point to point.

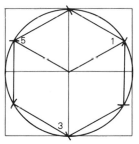

For Baby Blocks, start by drawing a hexagon. Then divide the hexagon into three equal diamonds as follows: draw a straight line from intersection point 1 to the centre; another line from intersection point 5 to the centre. Bottom of vertical centre line from centre to intersection point 3 acts as the other dividing line.

Semicircle/Quarter-circles

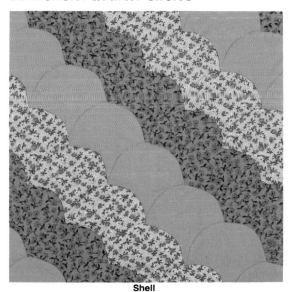

Shell

A semicircle and two quarter-circles produce the shape repeated in the *Shell* patchwork. To form the shell to a desired finished size, begin with a square the height and width of the shell (the most common actual size being 8 cm)

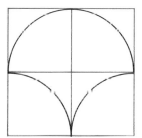

Draw a square and find its centre (Step 1, facing page). With pivot point of compass on centre, extend pencil leg along the horizontal centre line to side of square; form a semicircle in upper half of square. With compass at same setting, place pivot on lower left corner and form a quarter-circle, move pivot to lower right corner and form another quarter-circle.

Drunkard's Path

A quarter-circle smaller than a square is what must be drawn to produce the repeat in this pieced block design. The block begins with a square divided into a 4 × 4 grid; identical quarter-circles are drawn with compass, guided by 16-square grid.

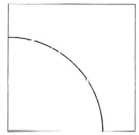

Draw a square; divide into a 4 × 4 grid (p. 24). With pivot of compass on corner of grid square, extend its pencil leg along one side of the square to a point about three-quarters along the side. Draw a quarter-circle by swinging the pencil to the opposite side. For templates, only one quarter-circle need be drawn. When designing, form a quarter-circle in each grid square, keeping the compass at a uniform setting; follow illustration on left for placement of quarter-circles.

Patchwork basics

Designing appliqué

The appliqué block units used most often consist of a **single** or **multiple-layer** appliqué and a square of base fabric. As the names imply, the first appliqué type consists of one layer of fabric, the second of several layers. Because of the one fabric layer limitation, single-layer appliqué can have only one colour and the shapes are usually those of simple, recognisable objects that you can trace or draw freehand. Maple Leaf is a single-layer appliqué. A more intricate design, such as the Snowflake, can be formed by cutting a design through a folded piece of paper (p. 7). Multiple-layer appliqué can have more than one colour; the designs, which can be drawn or traced, can be more realistic than single-layer designs. The Rose and the flowers in the Basket of Flowers are examples.

When designing appliqué, draw the base square and appliqué any size. It is only necessary to draw them to finished size at the template stage. The appliqué must fit within the square; some space can be left between the appliqué and the edges of the square as background.

There are two other types of appliqué block units. One consists of a **pieced** appliqué and a square of a base fabric.

The appliqué is designed to fit in the square; the area for the appliqué is sub-divided to form the shapes of the appliqué. An example is the Dresden Plate, see p. 26. The last type of appliqué block unit combines a single or multiple-layer **appliqué** with a **pieced block**. An example is the Basket of Flowers. To design such a unit, draw a square, subdivide it into a grid, and a form a pieced block design (pp. 24–25). This will form the basket part of the design. Then design an appliqué to fit an area of the block. The Basket of Flowers is based on a 6 × 6 grid, and the appliqué flowers fit its upper part.

Maple Leaf

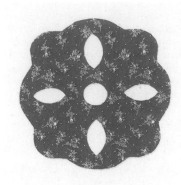

Snowflake

Rose

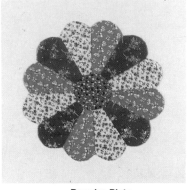

Dresden Plate

Basket of Flowers

Crazy patchwork

Crazy patchwork design is unique among pieced block patchworks in that the pieces that form the design are random sizes, shapes and colours. Originally, crazy patchwork was worked as one large block unit. An easier way of working is to sew the pieces to form small block units, then sew these blocks together. The only element that has to be exact in size and shape is the block of base fabric to which the pieces are sewn, this is decided during charting (p. 31). For a method of deciding the arrangement of the pieces, see right.

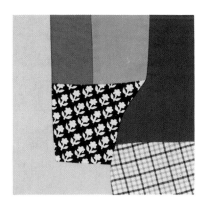

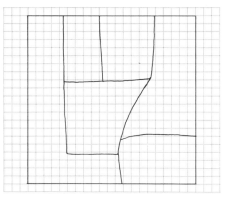

A sketch of an arrangement of shapes for one or all of the blocks can be helpful in designing and working a crazy patchwork. The most difficult aspect of crazy patchwork is imagining how random shapes will work together. By drawing an arrangement of shapes, you can see the design they form, and alter any of the shapes before they are cut out. You can even colour in the sketch to see how colours will work in the design. A tinted sketch can serve as both a shape and a colour guide when you are cutting out the pieces. If you like, you can make a finished-size replica of the sketch, cut it apart, and cut the fabric pieces from the paper pieces. Remember, if you do this, to add a 5 mm seam allowance to each piece.

Dividers and borders

Two other elements in patchwork are dividers and borders. Made of strips of fabric, they are joined to other patchwork units to become part of the overall patchwork fabric. Dividers are sewn between blocks and strips of blocks; borders are sewn to the outer edges of the joined patchwork units. The best time to plan for them is when you are charting the design (p. 31). It is then that you can see the needs of the overall patchwork design; you are also able to decide if the addition of a border or divider or both will produce a more desirable finished size for the patchwork. Although their main function is to 'frame' other patchwork units, an interesting patchwork fabric can be formed by sewing these strips to each other. This is known as a *strip quilt.*

Depending on the effect you want, the strips can be made of continuous fabric lengths or of pieced lengths. Strips made from continuous fabric lengths do not require finished-size templates; just calculate their length and width and add a 5 mm seam allowance at each edge. If necessary, plan to join lengths to achieve the measurement you require. Additional decoration can be supplied by appliqué. If using appliqué, decide where it will be placed and design it to fit that area. Appliqué will need finished-size templates.

Pieced fabric strips are made up of small and relatively simple pieced block units. To design a pieced strip, decide on a suitable block design and plan to repeat it for the length of the strip. Some designs are shown on the right; for more information, turn to pp. 24–25. While designing, pay attention to corners and other points where strips will meet. Some pieced designs will not match at these points; the easiest remedy is to use a plain square at corners or intersections. With other pieced designs, a different colour arrangement in the block will make the design work.

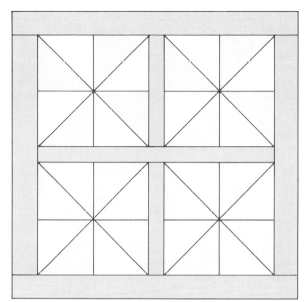

Continuous-strip dividers and borders are used in the patchwork above. They can be left plain (as above) or decorated with appliqué. Several examples of appliquéd strips are illustrated below.

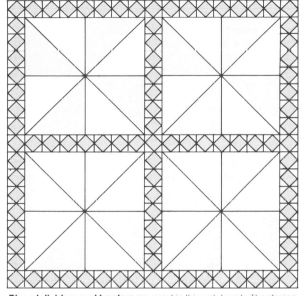

Pieced dividers and borders are used in this patchwork. The design of a pieced strip is formed by the repetition of a small pieced block. Notice the base block units outlined in the pieced strips below.

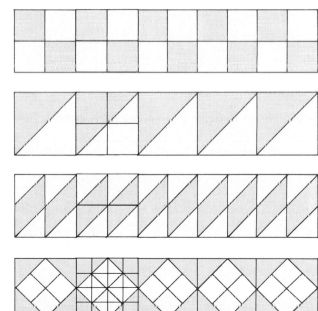

29

Patchwork basics

How colour can influence a patchwork design

Colour selection and arrangement are central to the overall design impression of a patchwork. It is simple to choose and arrange colours for a single pieced block, but for a multi-block patchwork you must consider the effect of colours on one another when many blocks are joined.

Choose colours carefully. Their arrangement depends on the area you want emphasised – whether you want the design of the *individual units* to stand out, or prefer to develop a *secondary overall pattern* from the combined units.

Supposing you like the idea of a secondary pattern, should it have more impact than the individual units? Or would you like to create the illusion of an interplay between the two, with first one and then the other predominant?

Getting the effect you want calls for experimentation with colours and their arrangement. A good way is to try out colour plans over a charted patchwork (see far right, opposite page). Bear in mind, as you do, these general colour theories as they apply to patchwork.

The dominant colours – reds, yellows and oranges – stand out more than do blues, greens and violets. Thus in combining, say, red and green, put red where you want emphasis.

Lighter tones, as a rule, show up more than darker ones, depending on the original colour they come from. Pink, derived from red, will stand out more than a comparable tone of blue. **The more space a colour covers,** the greater its strength will generally be.

Place emphasis in a patchwork *within* the units if you want their design more obvious; *at their edges* if you prefer to stress the secondary pattern. To equalise the two, balance colour strength and quantity among all pieces of all units.

Position of units, too, can affect a design's look. Notice below the dramatic result of setting blocks diagonally. On the opposite page, plain blocks and dividers separate the pieced blocks, emphasising their design but also creating another kind of secondary pattern.

Printed fabrics For patchwork, the small patterns are best. Small prints create an impression of dots. Prints with straight lines produce striping.

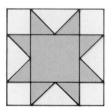

Concentration of one colour over the entire star shape gives that area great impact, strong enough for the block unit to remain dominant in the total design. The colour itself, being moderate in value and having yellow and red as its major components, contributes to this emphasis.

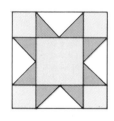

The colours here are balanced in mass and comparative impact; their weight evenly distributed over the patchwork piece. Let your eye move naturally from shape to shape, and you will perceive the play back and forth from unit design to secondary pattern.

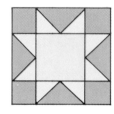

Blocks set on the diagonal, with strong colour emphasis at their edges, show the striking difference unit arrangement can make. The eye is drawn diagonally, making the secondary pattern more prominent than the unit design. It takes effort, in fact, to find the block design in the pattern.

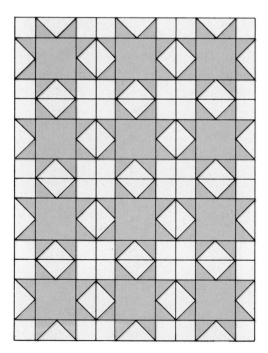

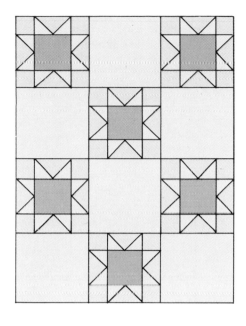

Alternating plain and pieced
blocks is undoubtedly the surest and easiest way to make unit designs stand out, if that is your preference. In every sense of the words, the plain blocks set the pieced blocks apart, giving them great clarity and definition. This idea is worth considering for a first try at design because it avoids the extreme colour reactions that can occur when pieced blocks are set edge to edge. The plain blocks could be a totally different colour from any in the unit design, but it is simpler and more effective to pick up one of those in the pieced block.

Dividers emphasise unit designs
as a frame does a painting. They are made of continuous fabric strips, but they could also be pieced (see p. 20). Dividers are often introduced into patchwork to bring it up to a required size. If you preferred to place the pieced blocks edge to edge, you could use borders instead of dividers to increase the size. It is also possible to combine the two. For details about these and other possibilities offered by borders and dividers, see p. 29. Techniques for joining them to blocks appear on pp. 44–45.

Charting a patchwork

Before actually charting a patchwork design, assign measurements to all the different units and see how they will fit into the approximate finished measurement of the patchwork. Then, if the combined measurements do not add up to near the desired finished size, alter the size or number of the units. Suppose, for example, you want your finished patchwork to measure approximately 2 m × 2.40 m and you plan to use five Simple Star blocks across by six down, with dividers between blocks and strips of blocks. If 30 cm blocks are used, they total 1.50 m × 1.80 m; if the dividers are 8 cm wide, the total is only 1.82 m × 2.20 m, smaller than the desired 2 m × 2.40 m. Add a 10 cm border, and the total measurement would be 2.02 m × 2.40 m, almost

exactly the right size. Another plan, which would produce exactly 2 m × 2.40 m is shown below. It uses larger (40 cm) but fewer blocks (four across by five down) and a 20 cm border. The blocks total 1.60 m × 2 m; the border brings the total to 2 m × 2.40 m.

If the combined units produce a satisfactory design, chart them to scale on graph paper and record the finished size of each. Then decide the best colour plan for the design. Place tracing paper over the chart and colour in all pieces. Use a new piece of tracing paper for each colour plan; leave the selected one on the chart. In buying fabrics, try to get as close a colour match as possible. Refer to the chart when making and using templates (pp. 32–33). Use the chart as a guide when you sew the patchwork.

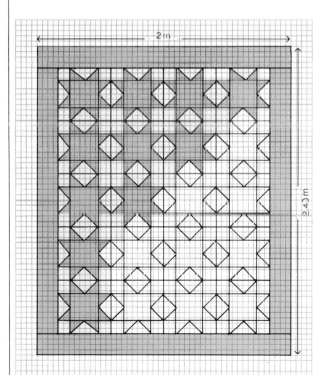

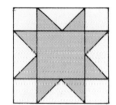

Finished size:
2 m × 2.40 m
Units:
20 Simple Star blocks each 40 cm square and coloured as shown

4 brown border strips, each measuring 20 cm × 2 m. (When cutting out, add 5 mm seam allowance to each side)

Preparing and sewing a block-unit patchwork

Making templates

The first step in the construction of a patchwork is to make a cutting and a marking template (pattern) for the different shapes in the design. To make templates of the correct size and shape, first draw to finished size each of the units in the patchwork that require templates. (All but crazy patchwork and continuous strip dividers or borders, pp. 28–29, will need templates.) For guidance in drawing patchwork units, see pp. 24–29. When units are drawn to finished size, study each one to determine the combination of shapes that can be most easily joined to form the unit's design. For example, when a Simple Star block is coloured as below, the first impression is of a one-piece star surrounded by separate triangles and corner squares. If you look more closely, you will see that the star, too, is composed of several pieces – namely, a large centre square, with small triangles making the points. Though it may seem otherwise, the second of the two combinations will be easier to join. To understand why, see p. 34 on choosing a joining sequence. When the shapes have been decided, make templates using sturdy paper or thin card (see below).

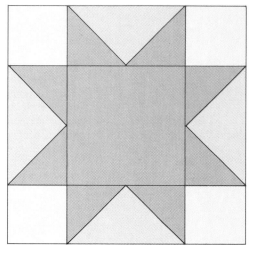

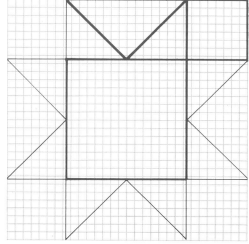

To make templates, proceed as follows:

1. On graph paper, draw the patchwork unit to its finished size.

2. Study the unit and determine the shapes that will need templates.

3. Carefully cut out one of each of the required shapes from the finished-size drawing. For example, the shapes needed for a Simple Star block are a large and a small square and a large and a small triangle. These shapes are indicated on the left by heavy lines.

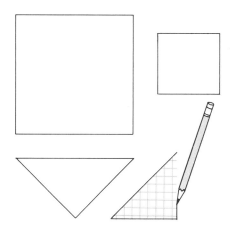

Marking templates

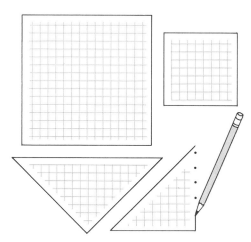

Cutting templates

4. Place cut graph-paper shapes on sturdy paper or thin card, trace around each. Remove shapes and cut out new pieces along traced lines. These are your *marking* templates.

5. Place graph-paper shapes back on the heavy paper, leaving 2 cm to 4 cm between them; tape in place. Mark several points 5 mm beyond each edge of each shape. Draw lines to connect marks; cut out new pieces along these lines. These are your *cutting* templates. The 5 mm between graph-paper shape and edge of template is the seam allowance needed to sew the pieces together.

Using cutting templates

Cutting templates are used first to determine the amount of fabric needed for a patchwork, then to cut out the pieces (see right).

Look at your charted patchwork and list the number of times each shape appears in each colour. Then, using one of the templates, see how many times it can be repeated across the fabric width (usually 90, 115 or 150 cm). Divide the number of times each shape appears in one colour by the number of units that fit across one fabric width; multiply the answer by the depth of one row (actually of one shape) to get the total length needed. Repeat for each shape; add the totals for each colour to determine the amount required of each. To allow for mistakes, always buy a little extra of each colour.

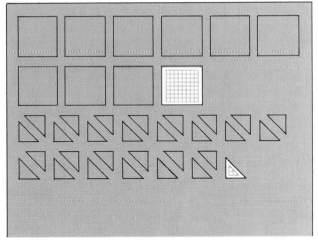
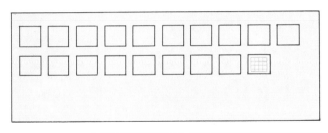
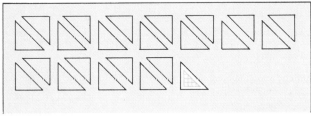

Place cutting template on wrong side of fabric and, using a dressmaker's pencil, draw its outline. Repeat until all of the pieces are drawn; be sure to draw the correct shape on the correct colour fabric. To save fabric, pieces can be drawn closer together than as shown here.

Special layout and cutting plans

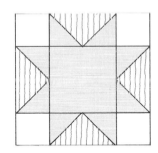
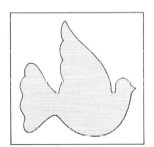

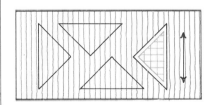

If using a one-way print fabric, such as a stripe, draw the shapes to reflect the direction you want the print to take in the finished block. Triangles were laid out as below so that the stripes would be as shown above in the finished block.

Shapes, too, can have a one-way direction. Two examples are the Dove appliqué (above, left) and the rhomboids in the Eight Point Star (above, right). When tracing the template of a one-way shape, place it on the wrong side of the fabric but in the direction opposite to its finished direction. The resulting cut piece, when it is turned to its right side, will face in the proper direction. The illustrations below show the shapes traced on the wrong side of the fabric, then the resulting cut shapes when turned to the right side.

Using marking templates

Marking templates are used in preparing cut fabric pieces for sewing; how they are used depends on the method of joining the pieces. Since most are joined with plain seams, a marking template is used mainly to mark seamlines (below). In appliqué pieces, marked seamlines are used as guides for staystitching and for turning seam allowances under; sometimes the marking template itself is used as a guide for pressing seam allowances back (p. 41). The marking templates of some one-shape patchworks are used to make paper pieces (p. 47).

To mark seamlines, centre marking template on wrong side of cut shape; hold it in place and, using a dressmaker's pencil, draw outline of marking template on fabric.

Preparing and sewing a block-unit patchwork

Choosing a joining sequence

Before doing any sewing, you must decide the best sequence to follow in putting the separate pieces together. With an appliqué block unit, you must decide on a layering sequence (p. 40). With a pieced block, you need a sequence for joining smaller pieces into progressively larger units. Look, first, for small units 'built' by repeated joinings of the same shapes. Then check the shapes adjoining these for another repeated joining that will make those small units larger. The small units, with additions, form strips that, when joined, produce many

blocks. Simple Star and Drunkard's Path, below, are examples. Some block designs are built from the centre (see the Eight Point Star, below).

Test whether your sequence will work by sewing one block. If it is not satisfactory, modify it until you find one that works, then follow it to sew all of the blocks simultaneously – that is, form all of the *smallest* units of all the blocks; then add the pieces that make them *progressively larger;* and finally, join the *larger strip units,* block by block, until all the blocks have been formed.

General sewing techniques

The pieces in a block unit may be joined with either hand or machine stitching. If it is an appliqué block, the appliqué is topstitched, usually by hand, to its base block (pp. 40–43). The pieces of pieced block units are generally joined with plain seams (exceptions: Log Cabin and Crazy blocks, pp. 38–39). **To form a plain seam,** place the pieces that are to be joined with right sides together and seamlines matched; pin and stitch through both layers on the seamline. Remove pins as you approach them; do not stitch over them. Hand-sew with a

small running stitch (see below); set the machine to short stitches. The thread colour should blend with fabric colours. The character of a seam – that is, whether straight, cornered or curved – will depend on the shapes of the pieces. (See straight seams below and on the facing page; cornered and curved seams on pp. 36–37.) Press seam allowances to one side (except certain cornered seam allowances, which are pressed open). At cross seams, alternate the direction of the seam allowances; this will distribute the bulk more evenly.

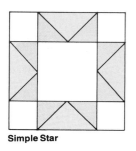
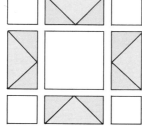

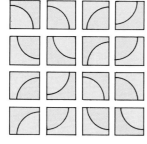
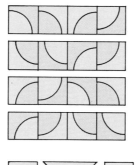

Simple Star

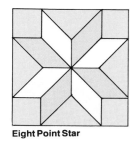
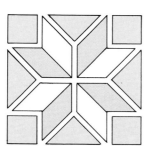
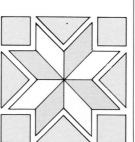

Drunkard's Path

Eight Point Star

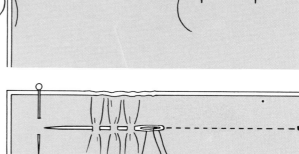

Machine sewing. Test stitch length, tension and pressure before starting to sew the blocks. Place stitches on seamline. Do not backstitch to secure stitches; tie thread ends if necessary (p. 36).

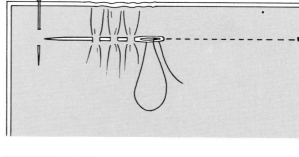

Hand sewing. Use running stitches. Weave needle in and out of fabric several times before pulling needle and thread through. Keep stitches and spaces between them short and even. Knot thread end to secure the start of the seam.

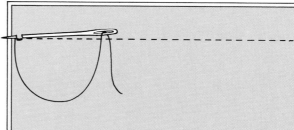

To secure the end of a seam, form a few small backstitches on top of each other.

Straight seams

A large proportion of all the pieces in pieced block designs have straight edges and will therefore be joined with plain straight seams. An example of a block in which all of the pieces are joined with straight seams is the Simple Star. This block consists of 17 pieces – a large centre square, four small corner squares, four large and eight small triangles. The pieces are joined in the sequence shown on the right.

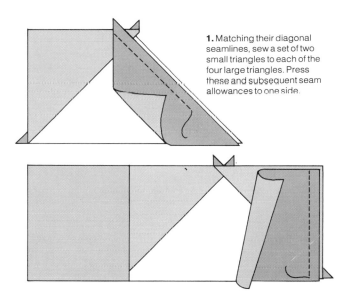

1. Matching their diagonal seamlines, sew a set of two small triangles to each of the four large triangles. Press these and subsequent seam allowances to one side.

2. To form the top and bottom strips of the Simple Star block, sew a small square to each end of two of the triangle units that were formed in Step 1 above.

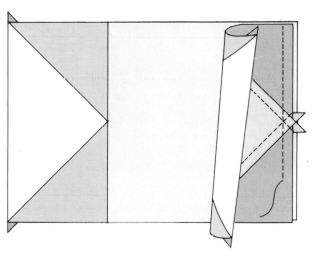

3. To form the centre strip of the block, sew the two remaining triangle units made in Step 1 to opposite edges of the large square. Take care to position the point of the large triangle and stitch across it exactly as shown above. This will ensure that the point of the triangle will be visible and will face towards the centre of the block when it is finished

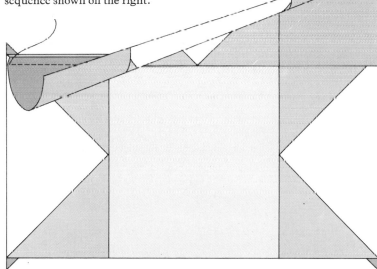

4. Sew the top strip to the centre strip. Match all cross seamlines and position and stitch across the point of the large triangle as was done in Step 3.

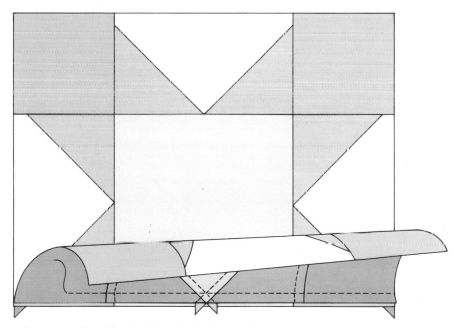

5. Complete the Simple Star block by sewing the bottom strip to the free edge of the centre strip. Be sure to match all cross seamlines and carefully position and stitch across the point of the triangle.

Preparing and sewing a block-unit patchwork

Cornered seams

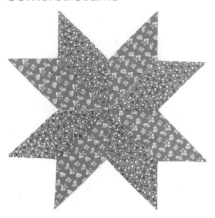

A cornered seam is used to join a piece having an outward-cornered edge to a piece with an inward-cornered edge. One will occur between each of the triangles and squares (outward corners) and the star unit (inward corners) of the Eight Point Star shown on this page. To prepare for a cornered seam, the inward corner is split; this allows the piece to be spread so its edges can be matched to the edges of the outward corner. If the inward-cornered piece, is formed by the seaming of two pieces (as happens in the Eight Point Star), the split will automatically be formed by stopping the seaming of the two pieces at the inward-cornered seamline (Steps 1, 3 and 4). If a *continuous piece of fabric* forms the inward corner, the corner will need to be stay-stitched and clipped (see the first column of the next page).

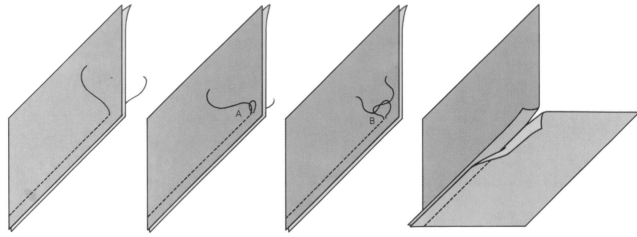

1. With long edges matched, sew a set of rhomboids together from edge of narrow corner to cross seam of wide corner. Pull top thread to bring up bobbin thread (A); tie together (B).

2. Form three more rhomboid units as explained in Step 1; press open the seam allowances of all four.

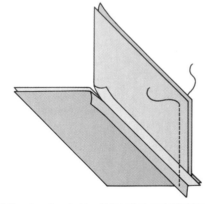

3. Sew two rhomboid units together; end stitching and tie threads as in Step 1. Press seam open. Sew remaining two units together the same way.

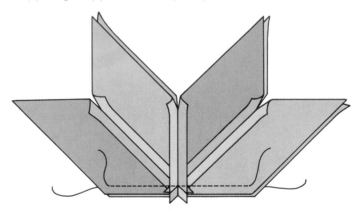

4. With right sides together, match seamlines and cross seams at lower edges of units made in Step 3; pin in place. Stitch units together, starting and stopping at the cross seamlines at each end of the matched units. Tie threads as in Step 1; press the seam open.

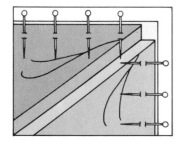

Squares and triangles are pinned and stitched to outer edges of star as follows. With right sides together and star uppermost, spread inward corner of star so its edges match those of piece being joined. Pin the two together, keeping seam allowances open.

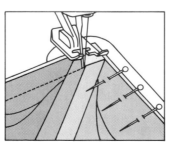

To sew first half of seam, stitch from edge of seam to corner; leave needle in fabric at corner. Lift presser foot; pivot fabric on needle to bring it into position for sewing the second half of the seam.

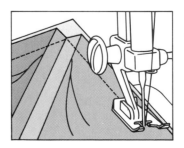

To sew second half of seam, lower presser foot and stitch from corner to end of seam.

If a continuous piece of fabric is used as the inward-cornered portion of a cornered seam, it must be reinforced with staystitching and clipped for flexibility as shown and explained below.

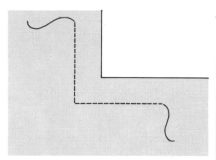

Reinforce the inward corner by placing a row of staystitching, just inside the seamline, for 2 cm on each side of the corner.

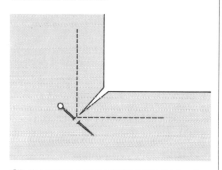

Clip the corner, being careful not to cut the staystitching. To avoid cutting these stitches, place a pin across the corner.

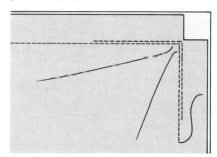

Spread clipped piece so its edges match those being joined to it. *Pin and stitch* through both layers as explained at bottom of facing page.

Curved seams

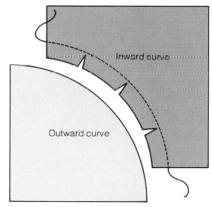

A curved seam is used when a piece with an outward-curved edge must be joined to one with an inward-curved edge. Such a seam forms each of the 16 small repeated units in the Drunkard's Path design illustrated here. To make the curved edges match, it is necessary first to staystitch and clip the inward-curved edge (Step 1). Then spread it to match the outward-curved edge and stitch through both layers on the seamline (see Step 2). To make the curved seams lie quite flat, press their seam allowances towards the inward curve. When all of the individual units have been stitched, they are joined to form four strips (Step 3); these strips are then joined with straight seams (Step 4).

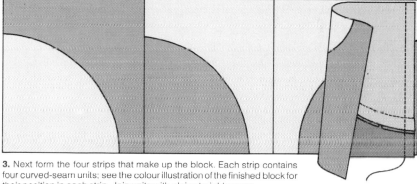

1. Prepare each inward-curved edge as follows: place a row of staystitching just inside the seamline. Then clip the seam allowance in a few places without cutting into the staystitching.

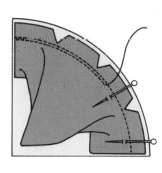

2. With right sides together and clipped piece uppermost, spread clipped edge to fit the outward curve. Pin and stitch along the seamline. Do the same for remaining 15 sets of pieces.

3. Next form the four strips that make up the block. Each strip contains four curved-seam units; see the colour illustration of the finished block for their position in each strip. Join units with plain straight seams.

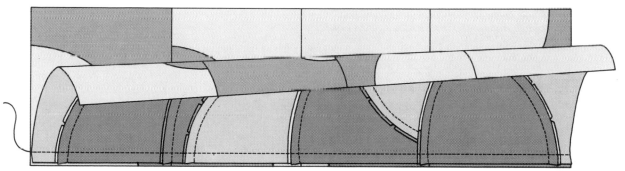

4. Sew the four strips to each other with plain straight seams, again referring to the coloured block for the position of individual strips. Be sure to match their cross seamlines exactly before stitching any of the strips together.

Preparing and sewing a block-unit patchwork

Seams through a base fabric/Log Cabin blocks

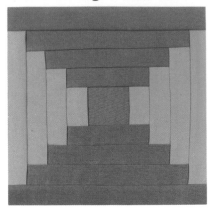

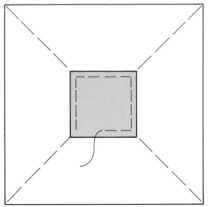

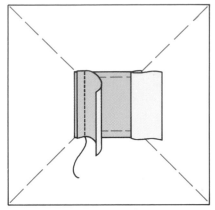

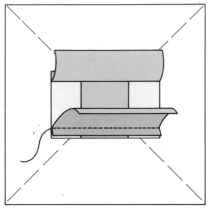

The pieces that make up Log Cabin blocks are seamed through a base fabric block as they are seamed to each other. Blocks are built from the centre out; the sewing sequence for the pieces (strips of graduated length) depends on the Log Cabin design. This design suggests an hour-glass.

1. Fold block of base fabric diagonally in half, then into quarters; lightly press folds. Open up block, mark the folds with tackings; then press block flat. With its right side up, centre the centre square of the pieced design on the block; use the tackings as guides for position. Pin and tack square to base block.

2. Sew the two shortest strips to opposite edges of the centre square. With right sides together, match, pin and stitch one strip to the right edge of square. Then turn the strip back to its right side and press it flat. Sew the other short strip to the left edge of the centre square. Turn it back to its right side and press it flat.

3. Sew the next larger set of strips to the top and bottom edges of the centre square and the strips sewn to it in the preceding step. Turn each strip to its right side and press flat. Continue sewing progressively larger sets of strips to the block, alternating their position from side to side, then to top and bottom. When all the strips have been sewn to the block, tack the free edges of the final strips to the base block of fabric.

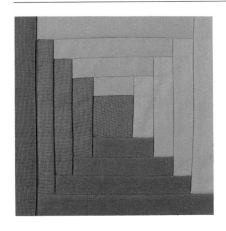

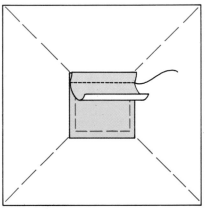

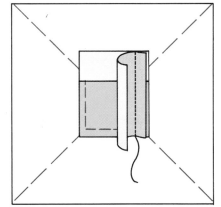

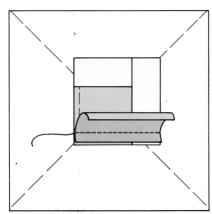

In another popular Log Cabin design, dark and light strips are grouped on opposite sides of a diagonal centre. The design here differs from the one shown above mainly in the sequence used for sewing the strips to each other through the base block of fabric (see right).

1. Mark base block of fabric and tack centre square in place as explained in Step 1 above. Then, with right sides together, match, pin and stitch the shortest light-coloured strip to the top edge of the centre square. Turn the strip to its right side and press it flat.

2. With their right sides together, match, pin and stitch the next longer light-coloured strip to the right edge of the centre square and the strip sewn to it in the preceding step. Turn the strip to its right side and press flat.

3. With their right sides facing, match, pin and stitch the shortest dark strip to the bottom edge of the centre square and the strip sewn to it in Step 2. Turn strip to its right side and press. Working clockwise, sew gradually longer sets of dark and light strips to block. End with the longest dark strip; turn and press each strip before sewing the next. Tack free edges of last round of strips to base block.

Seams through a base fabric/Crazy patchwork

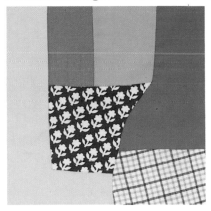

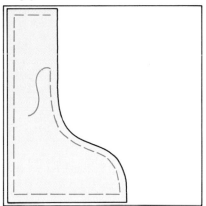

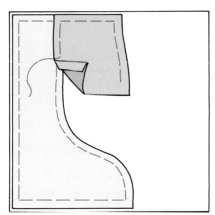

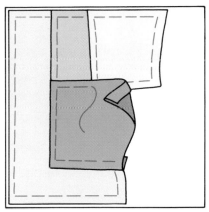

Crazy patchwork is different from other patchwork designs in that the only guide used for cutting the pieces is a sketch of the block's design (see p. 28). Also unique to crazy patchwork is the way in which the pieces are sewn to each other and to a base block of fabric (see the detailed instructions on the right).

1. Referring to your rough sketch of the block design (explained on p. 28), decide which piece should be laid down first. In general, it is best for the first piece to be laid along an edge of the block (left edge here). Cut a piece of fabric like the drawn shape, plus at least 5 mm seam allowance along each edge. Position the fabric piece, right side up, on base block of fabric; pin and tack it in place.

2. Decide which piece will be laid down next and cut a piece of fabric to that approximate shape, with 5 mm seam allowance along each edge. Position this piece, right side up, on the block, lapping it appropriately over the piece tacked in Step 1. Turn under the seam allowance of any lapped edge that will be exposed in the finished block; tack the piece in place along all of its edges. To turn under curved or cornered edges, see p. 41.

3. Continue to cut out and lap pieces one at a time and in the order of their relationship in the design. When cutting a piece, always remember to include 5 mm seam allowance along all of its edges; before tacking any piece in place, turn under the seam allowance of edges that will be exposed when the block is finished. When all of the pieces have been tacked in place, trim off any edges that extend beyond the edges of the base block.

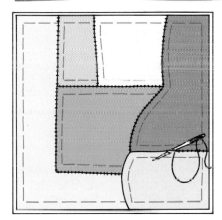

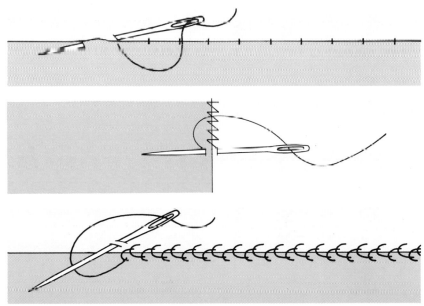

4. Secure each turned edge with hand stitches. If you want the stitches to be almost invisible, use either the slipstitch (p. 9) or the blindstitch, shown and explained on the right. For a more decorative finish, use the featherstitch (bottom right) or farmer's shirt stitch, to span both sides of the seamline. Finally, remove all tackings except at edges of block.

Blindstitch. Work stitches from right to left. Begin by bringing needle and thread through turned-under edge, back to front. Form stitches as follows: directly opposite point where thread comes out of folded edge, insert needle into block, take a small (about 5 mm) stitch, and bring needle out through turned-under edge. Pull needle and thread through, and repeat.

Farmer's shirt stitch. Hold seam vertical. To begin, bring needle and thread up on left side. Make a horizontal backstitch through the right side and bring the needle up the original hole. Make the next stitch a few threads down, from right to left, producing a slanted stitch. Continue making backstitches and slanting stitches.

Featherstitch. Hold seam vertical and work stitches down the seamline. To begin, bring needle and thread up on one side of seamline. Pass to opposite side, then, holding thread in place, point the needle diagonally down towards seamline and take a small stitch; keep thread under needle point. Pull stitch through, letting thread under it curve slightly. Cross to opposite side; repeat.

Preparing and sewing a block-unit patchwork

General techniques for patchwork appliqué

The first step in constructing an appliqué block unit is to make finished-size templates (p. 32) for all of the shapes in the appliqué as well as for the block if it is pieced (Basket of Flowers). If the base block is a continuous piece, no template is needed, only its finished measurement. Other elements, such as stems (in the Rose below) and the basket handle in the Basket of Flowers, can be made from bias fabric strips (p. 13). They are also exceptions and do not require templates; their finished measurements are sufficient.

Once all the pieces have been cut out and marked, the next step is to plan a **layering sequence,** that is, the order in which the pieces of the appliqué should be laid on top of each other. If it is a single-layer appliqué (for example, the Snowflake), no sequence is involved. For appliqué consisting of more than one layer, such as multiple-layer appliqué (Rose) or certain pieced appliqué (Dresden Plate), lay the pieces down in this order: the lowest layer first, and from the centre of the block out. Notice the sequence planned for the Rose

below. More examples of layering, as well as traditional construction techniques for appliqué block units, are given on pp. 42–43. For other appliqué methods, see pp. 6–20.

When planning a layering sequence, identify those edges that can be lapped under other pieces, and those that will be exposed and therefore must be turned under. The dotted lines in the schematic drawing of the Rose (below) signify lapped edges; all other edges will be turned under. It is usually easier to turn under the edges of the pieces before

they are positioned on the base block. When **turning an edge under,** turn it along its seamline and crease the seamline with either finger-pressing or an iron. If you have difficulty turning the edge, place a row of staystitching along the seamline or use the marking template as a pressing guide (next page). If the edge is cornered or curved, clip or notch it. After all the pieces have been tacked on to the block, hand-stitch the appliqué. Use either the slipstitch (p. 9), blindstitch or farmer's shirt stitch for a more decorative finish (p. 39).

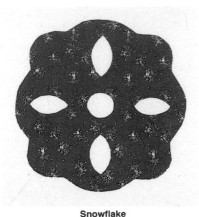

Snowflake

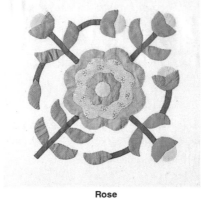

Rose

Dresden Plate

Basket of Flowers

Plan a layering sequence, that is, the order for laying down the pieces (indicated by numbers). Then decide which edges will be *overlapped* (dotted lines) and which *turned under* (all other edges).

Turning edges

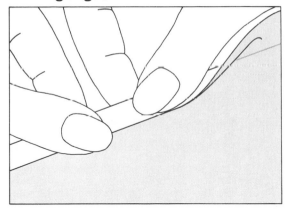

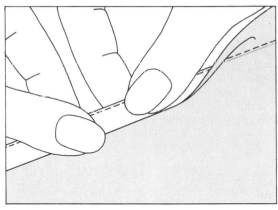

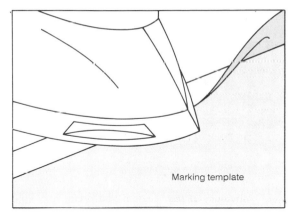

Marking template

Finger-pressing is one way of creasing a turned-under edge. Turn the edge under along its seamline, pressing the fold between your fingers as shown.

A row of staystitching placed just inside the seamline will make it easier to turn an edge under. While turning, use an iron or finger-pressing to crease the seamline.

A marking template can also be used as a guide for turning an edge under. Centre template on wrong side of piece and hold it in place. Then, using an iron, press edge back on to template.

Handling curves and corners

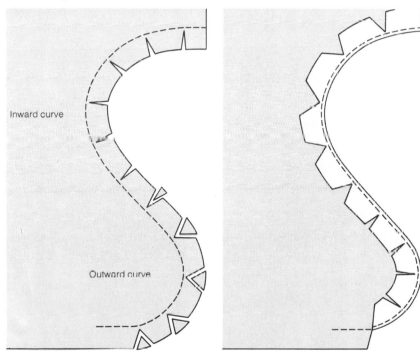

Inward curve

Outward curve

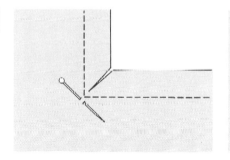

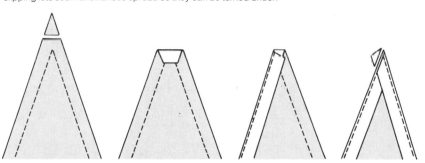

For an inward-cornered edge, first staystitch for at least 2 cm on each side of corner. Place a pin through stitches at corner, then clip up to the stitches. Pin keeps you from cutting into the stitches; clipping lets seam allowances spread so they can be turned under.

Curved edges will need to be either clipped or notched before they can be turned under; they should also be staystitched. If the edge has an *inward curve,* clip the seam allowance so it can be spread as the edge is turned. Notch an *outward curve* to reduce fullness and facilitate turning.

For an outward-cornered edge, first staystitch for at least 2 cm on each side of corner. Trim half of the seam allowance across the corner; then turn the remainder back across point of corner. Then, one at a time, turn back the seam allowance on each side of the corner; trim any excess seam allowances.

Preparing and sewing a block-unit patchwork

Single-layer appliqué block units

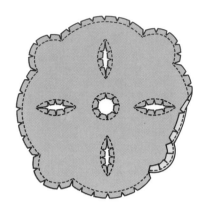
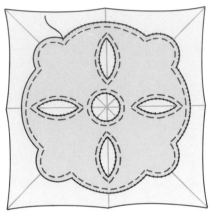

Appliqué block units involving a single-layer appliqué, such as the Snowflake above, are easy to construct. The only pieces called for are one fabric layer for the appliqué and one for the base block. All edges of such an appliqué will need to be turned under.

1. Using the methods described on p. 41, turn under all the edges of the appliqué. Since all the edges of this appliqué are curved, they should all be staystitched; then edges that have inward curves should be clipped and those with outward curves should be notched.

2. Fold base block of fabric in half, then into quarters. If parts of the appliqué must be centred diagonally, as do the four 'corners' of appliqué above, fold block into eighths as well. Lightly press all folded edges; open up block. Using foldlines as guides, centre the appliqué on the block. Pin and tack appliqué in place from centre out. Be sure to catch the turned-under edges in the tackings.

3. Working from the centre of the appliqué out, hand-sew the appliqué to the base block. If you want the stitches to be almost invisible, use either the slipstitch (p. 9) or blindstitch (p. 39) and a thread colour that matches the appliqué. For a more decorative finish, use an embroidery stitch; thread colour can match or contrast. Remove the tackings and press.

Multiple-layer appliqué block units

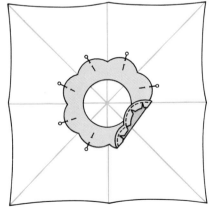
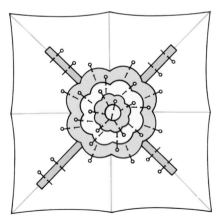

Before constructing a multiple-layer appliqué block unit, for example, the Rose above, plan a layering sequence for the appliqué pieces. When the sequence has been decided, identify the edges that can be lapped under other pieces and those that will need to be turned under.

1. Prepare all the pieces of the appliqué. Referring to its planned layering sequence (p. 40) and using the methods on p. 41, turn under only those edges that will be exposed. Form centring guidelines on the base block of fabric by folding it in quarters, and eighths if necessary (see Step 2 above). Begin to lay down and pin the pieces to the base block according to the planned sequence.

2. Continue to lay down the pieces of the appliqué according to the planned layering sequence, pinning each piece in place. If necessary, lift an edge so another can be lapped under it (as happens above with each stem at the edge of the centre rose).

3. When all the pieces have been pinned to the block, tack them in place. Remove pins as you tack, and work the tackings from the centre of the appliqué out to its edges. Then hand-sew the appliqué to the block as explained in Step 3 above.

Pieced appliqué block units

Some appliqué block units, such as the Dresden Plate, employ pieced block techniques to form all or part of the appliqué design. If more than one layer is involved, as is the case with the Dresden Plate, plan a layering sequence and determine which edges need turning.

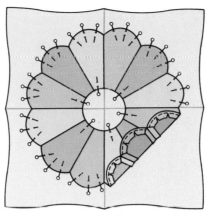

1. Construct the pieced appliqué, using pieced block techniques (pp. 34–39). Choose those seaming techniques that are suited to the character of the pieces being joined; wherever possible, press seams open. The pieced portion of the Dresden Plate appliqué (above) is formed by means of plain straight seams; all of the seams are pressed open.

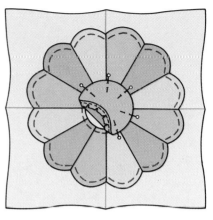

2. Referring to the layering sequence and using the techniques on p. 41, turn under the necessary edges of the appliqué. For Dresden Plate, the edge of the centre circle and outer edges of pieced portion need to be turned; before turning, each curved edge is staystitched, then clipped or notched. Form centring guides on the base block (Step 2, top of opposite page). Begin to lay down and pin pieces to block.

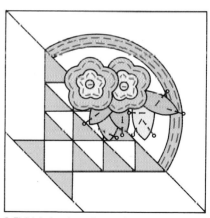

3. When all of the pieces have been pinned to the base block of fabric, tack them in place, removing the pins as you tack. When tacking, be sure that the turned-under edges are caught in the stitching. Then hand-sew the appliqué to the block as described in Step 3 at the top of the opposite page. Remove all tackings and press.

Appliqué-pieced block units

Certain appliqué block units combine a pieced block with a single or multiple-layer appliqué. Basket of Flowers is an example. Base block, including bottom of basket, is pieced; flowers and basket handle in the upper half of the block are a multiple-layer appliqué.

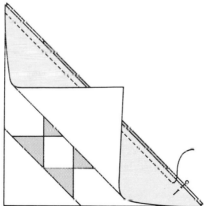

1. Construct the pieced base block, using the appropriate pieced block techniques (see pp. 34–39). Plain straight seams are used to join all the pieces in the block above; pairs of triangles are its smallest repeated unit. The lower half of the block is pieced first, and is then sewn to the upper half, which is a large triangle.

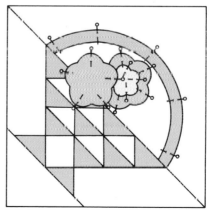

2. Refer to the planned layering sequence (p. 40) and turn under the appropriate edges of the appliqué, using the methods on p. 41. If necessary, fold the block to form centring guidelines (Step 2, top of opposite page). Begin to lay down the pieces of the appliqué; pin each in place. The basket handle is a bias fabric strip that has been shaped into a curve (p. 13).

3. Finish laying down the appliqué pieces, pinning each in place. When all are pinned to block, tack each in place. Remove pins as you tack; be sure to catch the turned-under edges in the tackings. Then hand-stitch the appliqué to the block (see Step 3, top of opposite page). Remove tackings and press.

Preparing and sewing a block-unit patchwork

Joining blocks, dividers and borders

In general, the best order for joining blocks, dividers and borders to form a patchwork fabric is as follows. Sew the units to form strips; sew the strips to each other; add the borders last. To determine how a particular patchwork should be formed, study its chart and mentally group the units into strips. In most designs, the strips go *across* the patchwork (see examples, immediate right). If vertical dividers are included, strips will be vertical (facing page, top left); in a diagonal setting (facing page, right), they will be diagonal.

The elements in a strip will depend on the units to be used and their arrangement in the design. If a patchwork is blocks only, the strips will be the same. If only vertical or only horizontal dividers are used, there will be, in addition to the strips of blocks, strips for the dividers. If *both* vertical and horizontal dividers are included (facing page, bottom left), there will be strips composed of blocks and vertical dividers and also strips for horizontal dividers.

Finishing techniques for any patchwork will depend on the item being made; refer to the Quilting chapter on pp. 71–75.

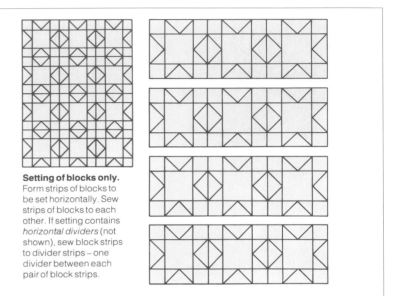

Setting of blocks only. Form strips of blocks to be set horizontally. Sew strips of blocks to each other. If setting contains *horizontal dividers* (not shown), sew block strips to divider strips – one divider between each pair of block strips.

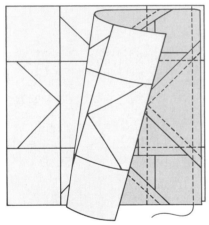

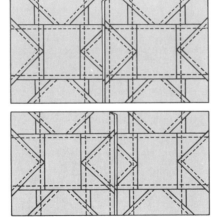

1. Join units to form strips. The number of units in a strip and the number of strips will depend on the planned patchwork. When joining units, use 5 mm seams; match cross seamlines.

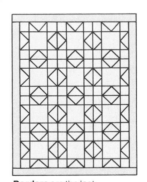

2. Press seam allowances between units to one side; alternate the direction from strip to strip. For example, press all in one strip to left, all in the next strip to the right.

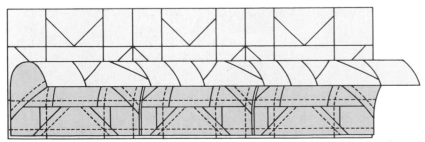

3. Join strips to each other according to the planned patchwork design. When joining the strips, use 5 mm seams and be sure to match cross seamlines. Press these seam allowances down.

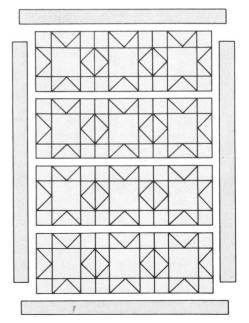

Borders are the last strips to be added to any patchwork. After all of the other units have been joined, sew a border strip to each edge of the patchwork – first to the right and left edges, then to the top and bottom.

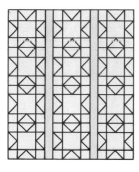

With vertical dividers. Form strips of blocks and divider strips to be set vertically. Sew the blocks of strips to the vertical divider strips, with one divider strip between each pair of block strips.

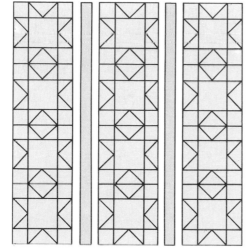

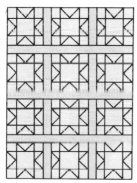

With both vertical and horizontal dividers. Join blocks and short vertical dividers in such a way as to form horizontal strips with a vertical divider between each pair of blocks. Next form horizontal divider strips. Sew the horizontal block strips to the horizontal dividers, with one divider strip between each pair of horizontal block strips.

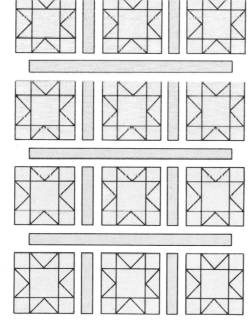

Diagonal setting. Here units are joined to each other to form strips that will be set diagonally. The number of units in a strip will depend on the location of that strip in the patchwork. Parts of units (necessary to permit all edges of the patchwork to be straight when all the strips are joined) are usually required at the ends of strips; some strips only contain part of a unit. Shown below is the strip breakdown of the patchwork on the right. Notice that each strip is different from the others, and that the upper right corner is formed by a quarter of a block and the lower left corner by two diagonally halved blocks. The numbers next to the strips indicate a suggested sequence for joining the strips.

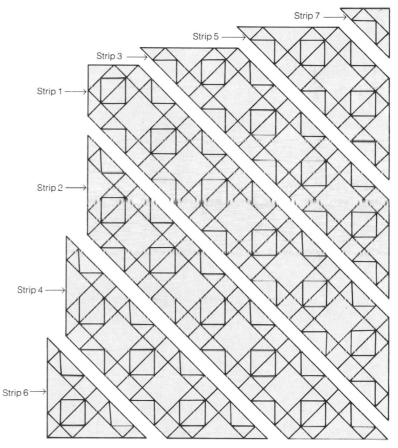

Strip 7
Strip 5
Strip 3
Strip 1
Strip 2
Strip 4
Strip 6

Preparing and sewing a one-shape patchwork

Preparatory steps
Shell
Baby Blocks
Grandmother's Flower Garden

Preparatory steps

The Shell, Baby Blocks and Grandmother's Flower Garden (hexagon) are three popular one-shape patchworks; for instructions on how to draw their necessary shapes, see p. 27. Many of the preparatory steps taken for a one-shape patchwork are the same as those taken for a block-unit patchwork. A one-shaped patchwork should be charted and its colour arrangement planned (pp. 30–31). Once charting is complete, finished-size marking and cutting templates can be made and the pieces cut out of the appropriate colours of fabric (pp. 32–33). If you are making the **Shell** patchwork (below), use its marking template to mark the seamlines of each shell shape. For **Baby Blocks** or **Grandmother's Flower Garden,** use the marking template as a pattern for cutting out finished-size paper shapes.

Shell

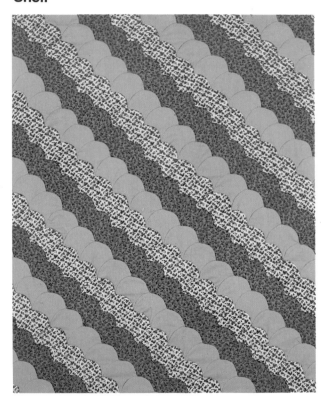

Many different colour arrangements can be used with the Shell patchwork; the one above produces diagonal stripes. If you want the outer edges of the patchwork to be straight, place partial shell shapes at the edges. Make marking and cutting templates for them, and sew them as you would full shells. Turn under the seam allowances of the edges that form the patchwork's edges.

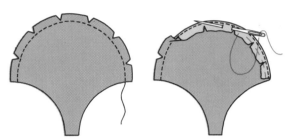

1. Staystitch and notch (p. 41) the upper seam of each shell shape. Turn each upper seam allowance to the wrong side and tack it in place.

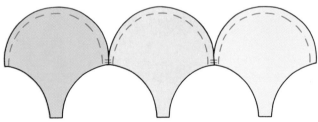

2. Referring to chart for colour, place top row of shells next to each other. Tack shells to each other, forming tacks within lower seam allowances.

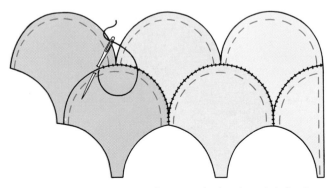

3. For each successive row, overlap appropriately coloured shells along lower curved seamlines of shells just positioned. Blindstitch (p. 39) in place.

Baby Blocks

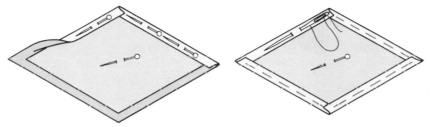

1. Using marking template as a pattern, cut out a paper diamond for each fabric diamond. Back each fabric diamond as follows. Centre a paper diamond on wrong side of fabric diamond. Turn seam allowances under and tack in place, through paper.

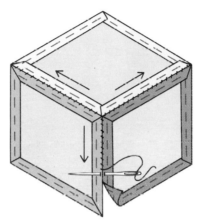

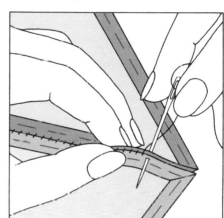

2. Form each Baby Block as follows. Position a set (3) of diamonds as shown in the far left illustration and sew them together, working from the centre of the Baby Block out. When sewing, hold the diamonds with their right sides together and oversew the matched edges neatly as shown in the illustration on the left.

When colours are appropriately chosen and placed, Baby Blocks patchwork produces the overall effect of three-dimensional blocks. The simplest way to achieve this effect is with three tones of one colour, placed in the same position in each block (Step 2). The Baby Blocks above combines three tones of brown, with the lightest at the top of the block, the darkest at the left, and the medium tone to the right. If you want the patchwork to have straight edges, use part shapes (see Shell, facing page).

3. Using small stitches (Step 2), oversew Baby Blocks to each other to form strips. Check chart for number of strips and of blocks in a strip. Oversew the strips together to form the patchwork. When stitching is done, remove paper backing pieces.

Preparing and sewing a one-shape patchwork

Grandmother's Flower Garden

Patchwork made from hexagons is easy to work, as each 'flower' shape can be sewn separately and joined to the others to make a quilt. All quilts look better if the arrangement of the colours in the hexagons is planned and not developed haphazardly. In this example, the orange centres to the 'flowers' and the white 'paths' between draw the whole quilt together, even though the groups of hexagons are made up of different colours and prints. Cardboard templates last for a long time, and must be cut with a metal ruler and utility knife.

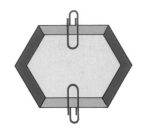

Cut the hexagons of fabric using a cutting template. Place the cardboard template hexagon centrally on the wrong side of the fabric.

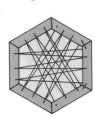

With needle and cotton begin to sew opposite sides together, pulling the thread tightly to 'lace' them together. Keep the stitches spaced evenly.

Fold the fabric over the template and use paper clips to keep the template in the centre of the fabric before sewing.

A completed hexagon showing the sides securely laced together. If the fabric is springy, take an extra stitch at corners. When sewn to six other hexagons, remove template.

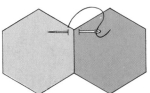

Sew the hexagons using farmer's shirt stitch, picking up the fabric with the needle but not piercing the cardboard templates. Make a backstitch and then insert the needle below.

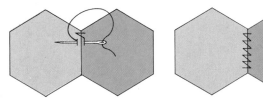

Pull the thread through, making a slanting stitch, and make a backstitch from right to left. Repeat. The diagram on the right shows the finished seam, which is both strong and decorative.

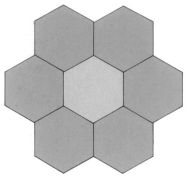

Make a 'flower' by surrounding one hexagon with six others of the same fabric. Sew each hexagon to the centre hexagon, and then to each other.

Make several 'flowers' of two circles of hexagons, combining colours and prints to make each attractive in itself. Then arrange them, to balance the colours and prints used, and join with a 'pathway' of white hexagons. The 'pathway' could alternatively be made of black fabric for a rich, dark effect.

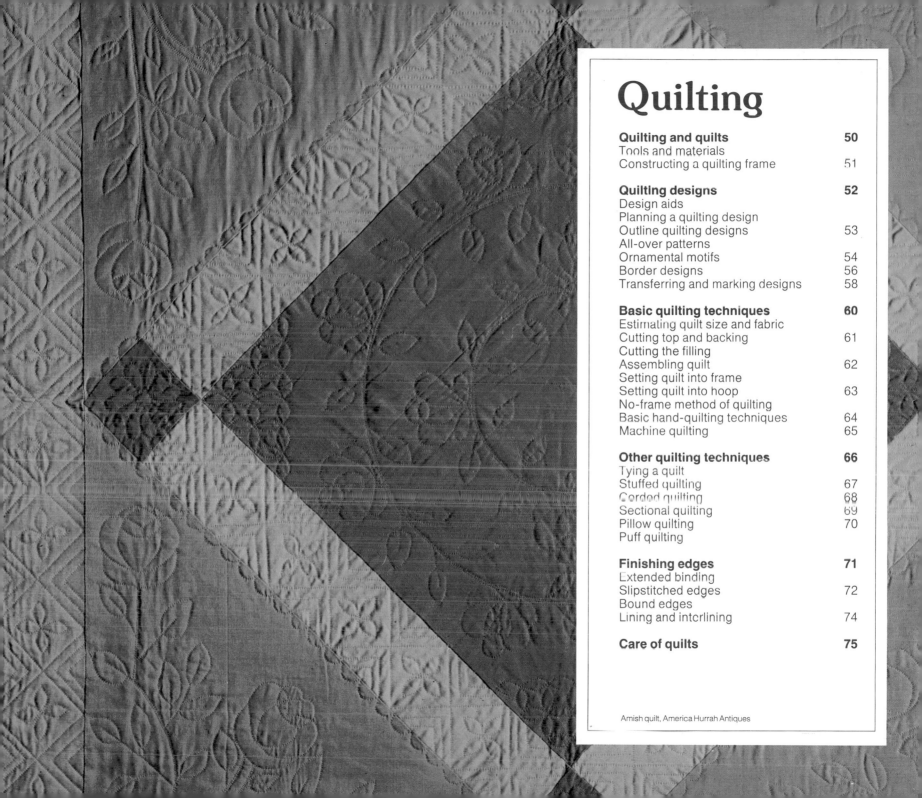

Quilting

Amish quilt, America Hurrah Antiques

Quilting and quilts

Introduction to quilting
Tools and materials
Constructing a quilting frame

Introduction

Quilting, like so many needlecraft techniques, is centuries old. Throughout history it has been valued as a source of warmth in such forms as clothing and bed quilts. The basic quilting technique involves simple running stitches used to anchor a soft filling between two layers of fabric. These stitches are usually worked in a systematic pattern to create a subtly textured fabric surface. The quilting patterns (see pp. 53–57) may be the primary or only source of decoration on a particular article, or they may be a secondary source that is introduced to enhance a completed design surface, such as patchwork or appliqué.

Although this basic quilting technique is usually associated with the making of a quilt (or bed covering), it is often decoratively applied today to sections of such garments as jackets, waistcoats and dressing-gowns. Quilting is also suitable for decorating such accessories for the home as cushions and wall hangings.

Ornamental motif quilted on plain fabric is quilt's primary design source.

Outline quilting merely enhances the main patchwork design of this quilt.

Tools and materials

Fabrics and filling. The top layer or decorative side of a quilted project can be a plain or patterned fabric, or it can be a completed piece of patchwork, appliqué or embroidery. Whatever it is, the fabrics used should be smooth, light to medium-weight and opaque. Cotton, poplin and polyester/cotton are popular choices, although fine linen-weave fabrics or flannels are also suitable. Rich fabrics such as velvet, satin and silk can also be used for special quilted projects. For a delicate effect, use sheer fabric (voile, organdy, organza) as a transparent overlay on an opaque top. Avoid heavy or stiff fabrics; they are not suitable. Bed sheets are convenient to use as they are made in a wide range of colours and prints, and in widths that make it possible to have a conveniently large seamless piece. Sheeting may also be bought by the metre.

The bottom layer, backing or lining, traditionally has been a utilitarian medium-weight fabric such as calico. Nowadays, it, too, is likely to be decorative, and made from fabrics as bright in pattern and colour, and similar in type and style to the top fabric layer. Avoid any slippery fabric, as the quilt will slide off the bed.

If the backing will also be the binding (see p. 71), you will need to cut it larger than the quilt top. Before quilting, preshrink all fabrics for both the top and the bottom.

The most common filling is synthetic wadding, manufactured in sheet form. It is washable, lightweight, warm and easy to quilt. It gives an attractive, plump quilted surface. It is available in a variety of thicknesses and widths. Good-quality synthetic wadding is uniformly thick and dense, which makes it easy to handle when assembling a project. Try to buy wadding that is large enough to be used as a single piece. If the wadding is too small, you can join two pieces to produce one of the desired size (see p. 61). Cotton wadding is available, but as it is not washable it is only suitable for items such as spectacle cases, which do not need laundering.

Old blankets may be used as wadding. Avoid using parts that have been worn thin, as the quilting will be uneven.

Traditionally, teased sheep's wool was used. This would make a very warm filling if used for a garment such as a child's waistcoat.

Needles, thread and hand-sewing aids. *Quilting needles*, which are also known as 'betweens', are the usual choice. As a rule, the sizes are 8 or 9, but a heavier size 7 can be used on heavier quilt fabrics, and a finer number 10 can be used on fabrics that are delicate.

Thread for quilting must be strong. Cotton thread coated with a 'glaze' is sometimes labelled *quilting thread* and does the job well. A good, all-purpose thread, number 50 or coarser number 40, can also be used; you may want to run each strand of thread through a cake of *beeswax* to help prevent tangles and fraying as you work. For a richer look, use a lustrous silk twist.

A *thimble* that fits your finger snugly is very helpful, as are small *embroidery scissors* for cutting thread.

Frames and hoops. When quilting is put in a frame or hoop the material is stretched taut, and the stitching done under tension. When removed, this produces a plump look which is most attractive. For quilting large expanses of fabric, a quilting frame is most convenient.

A simple but strong frame is shown below. If you decide to make many quilts, it is worth getting a frame made by a local handyman or carpenter. Traditional frames were rectangles made of end rails and stretchers, and were placed on the backs of kitchen chairs when being used. Pine is the most usual wood, although oak and mahogany frames may be seen in museums.

Although a frame is the most convenient method for a large piece, it takes up space. Many people prefer to use a hoop. These are available up to 56 cm wide. This size will hold the quilting layers securely and can be adapted for any size quilting project. To use a hoop on a large quilt, shift it from area to area. The hoop should be at least 45 cm in diameter to provide a practical working area. You may like to look for a hoop with a stand which leaves both hands free. A hoop made for embroidery will not be suitable, as the two hoops will fit together too tightly to take the sandwich of fabric and wadding.

However, if you are a beginner, and wish to experiment with a fairly small piece of quilting, you can work the piece in your hands, without a hoop. If you do this, remember to tack the layers together very securely so that they will not slip while quilting.

Quilting hoops come in several diameter sizes; select one appropriate for your project. This model comes with a convenient stand, and frees both hands for work.

Constructing a quilting frame

A sturdy quilting frame can easily be constructed at home by following the instructions below. When not in use, it can be taken apart and stored.

Materials

To make the frame, you will need four lengths of 25 mm × 50 mm wood that have been sanded smooth to prevent any snagging of the quilt fabric. Two of the lengths will be used as *rails* around which the quilt will be rolled. Each rail should equal the width of the quilt, plus 30 cm to allow for clamping at corners. The two remaining lengths will act as side *stretchers*; a length of approximately 60 cm to 90 cm, plus another 30 cm to allow for clamping, should be adequate for most projects. You will also need about eight 15 cm *G-cramps*, and two strips of *webbing, ticking* or other sturdy fabric about 5 cm to 8 cm wide and as long as the cut rails. *Staples* or *drawing pins* are needed to hold the ticking or webbing to the rails. Support the frame with two *trestles*.

Assembly

To assemble the frame, first attach a strip of webbing or folded ticking to each rail as shown below. (Ends of quilt will be sewn to webbing when quilt is set into frame.) Position the four lengths at right-angles to each other with the rails resting on top of the stretchers. Secure lengths together with a G-cramp at each outside corner. Raise the frame on to the trestles, placing it so that the stretcher bars lie directly on the trestles. Hold the frame steady with additional G-cramps. Set the quilt into the frame, following the procedure described on pp. 62–63.

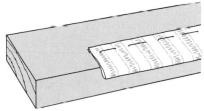

To attach fabric strip, fold and staple or tack to long edge of rail. Use webbing singly.

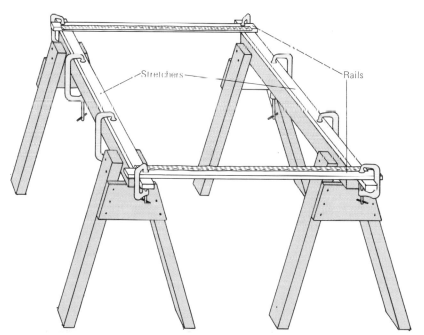

Stretchers

Rails

To assemble frame, clamp rails to stretchers at corners. Position frame so the stretchers rest on the trestles, then clamp trestles and stretchers together as shown.

Quilting designs

Design aids

A wide range of accessories exists to help with designing, or with the transfer of designs, but not all of them will be needed for any single project. What you select depends upon your design, and the transfer method it requires.

Patchwork templates or ready-made stencils, sold for interior decorating, can be used to make quick and easy quilt designs. You can make your own if you need or wish to (see p. 59).

Planning a quilting design

There are many different kinds of quilting designs, each offering a particular look or effect (see pp. 53–57). In deciding which one (or ones) to use, you must first consider the top fabric layer. Then, with that in mind, plan the quilting design so that it both enhances the piece and maintains its original character. In general, an already patterned top layer (such as patchwork or an appliquéd top) will be most appealing with simple, unobtrusive quilting. A common design practice is merely to quilt around the shapes that are already there. Elaborate quilting designs, on the other

There are several kinds of paper that will help with planning and transfer. *Graph paper* is useful for planning or sketching a design to scale. For full-size quilting designs and perforated patterns, *tracing paper* is the best choice. Use a stiff, *sturdy paper*, manila card or cardboard, to make durable templates and stencils. *Dressmaker's carbon* is handy for transferring markings.

A *ruler* or *metrestick* will double as a

hand, stand out most attractively against plain, solid colours. In fact, the most detailed quilting designs often appear on plain white quilts. A typical antique quilt of this sort may feature an ornate central motif surrounded closely by smaller motifs and an overall quilted background. Sometimes a single quilting project may combine both of these design approaches. For example, an intricately quilted solid-colour border may be used around a patchwork top quilted in a simple style.

The type of filling can also influence your quilting plans. Of the fillings previ-

straight-edge for marking straight-line designs and as a measuring device. A *compass* or a *round object* (such as a teacup) can be used for drawing curves. A single-edged *razor blade* or a *craft knife* will cut stencils and templates accurately. To mark directly on fabric, use a hard *pencil* or *dressmaker's chalk*. A special powder called *pounce* is used for temporary markings with perforated patterns.

ously mentioned (p. 50), cotton wadding is the least stable, and should be closely quilted to prevent the wadding from shifting and separating into unsightly lumps. Far less quilting is needed to anchor synthetic wadding, or any of the more stable fillings; with these, as much as a 25 cm square can be left unquilted. If you want a comparatively flat overall surface, plan on a closely quilted piece, whether the filling is cotton or polyester. Widely spaced quilting designs hold the filling down less, and so will result in a plumper surface.

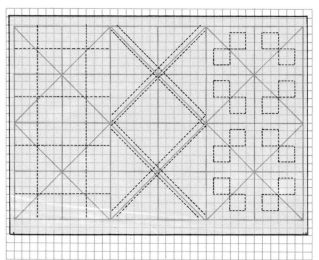

To plan a design for a quilt or any large expanse of fabric, sketch the proposed design on graph paper.

For patchwork, first draw the completed patchwork design on graph paper, then lay a sheet of tracing paper on top and sketch a quilting plan over the drawing as shown. Try several quilting plans in this way, and select the one you feel most enhances the patchwork.

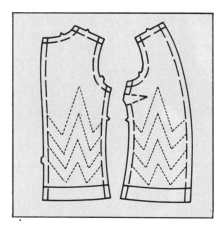

For clothes, plan quilting design on traced pattern pieces. Match quilting at seamlines. Remove wadding from darts before making up the garment.

Types of quilting designs/Outline quilting

Outline quilting follows the outlines of existing shapes. Patchwork, appliqué and patterned fabrics are suitable for this type of quilting. Position quilting lines about 5 mm from the seamed edges of stitched down shapes or the outer edge of printed motifs.

Each shape can be outlined as in the first illustration; every patch in design is quilted.

Selected areas can be quilted to emphasise certain aspects of a design. In the second illustration the 8-sided star is accentuated by quilting around the patches that form the star.

In echo quilting, the outline of a shape is repeated in concentric quilting lines. This technique is often used for appliquéd tops.

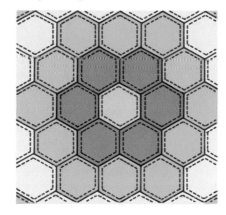 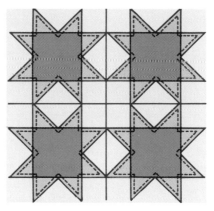 

Types of quilting designs/All-over patterns

All-over quilting produces a regular pattern by consistent repetition of one or more shapes. Designs can be adapted to any space, and so are widely used. They can be used to cover an entire surface with a simple, unobtrusive quilted background, or to fill open areas around or within other quilted motifs.

Straight-line designs are the easiest patterns to use; they can be drawn using just a metrestick or ruler. A simple vertical pattern is shown in the first illustration.

Criss-crossed diagonals produce a pattern of diamond shapes in the second illustration.

Diamond shapes surround and emphasise a central motif in the third illustration.

All-over curved patterns make interesting background designs. Templates of stiff paper are used in repeat to create the patterns. Some patterns are formed by overlapping one or more templates; notches are cut along template curve to indicate overlapping points.

Shell pattern in first illustration calls for the simple repetition of a single template.

Overlapping circles in next illustration are marked with one round template, notched to indicate overlapping points of circles.

Crescent pattern is formed by using round templates in two sizes. A predetermined arc on each one is used to mark the top and bottom curves of the crescent shape.

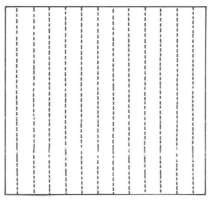 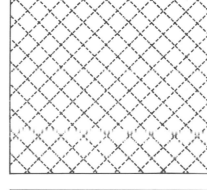 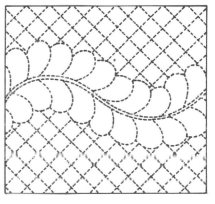

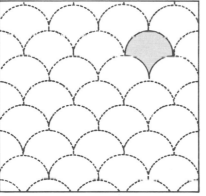 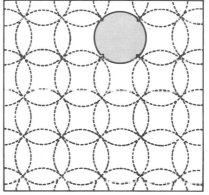 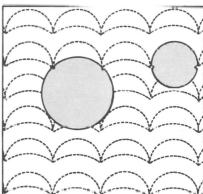

Quilting designs

Types of quilting designs/Ornamental motifs

Another type of quilting design is the ornamental motif, which depicts traditional subjects in a somewhat formal fashion. These motifs usually contain intricate details (see illustrated examples) that can best be seen and appreciated when they are worked on plain fabric surfaces. In many of the most elegant quilts from earlier periods, the larger, more elaborate designs act as a central motif; smaller motifs may surround the centre design, perhaps deco-

rate the corners as well. If you would prefer to combine two or more motifs in a single piece, work out your design ideas first on graph paper. A single ornamental motif is a satisfactory way of decorating individual patchwork blocks or cushion covers. These patterns for ornamental quilting designs can be used, or you can make your own perforated patterns (p. 59). Quilt the tight curves that are typical of the designs with very fine stitches.

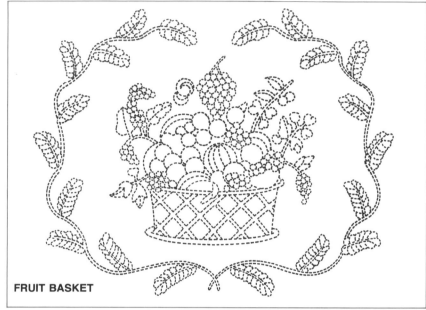

FRUIT BASKET

VASE OF FLOWERS

PINEAPPLE

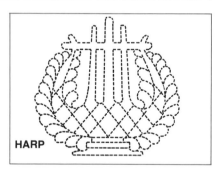

HARP

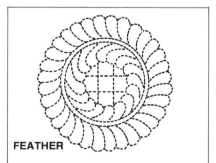

FEATHER

BUTTERFLY

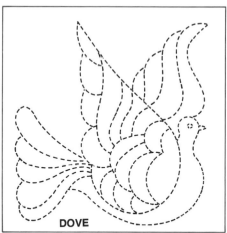

DOVE

TULIP

EAGLE

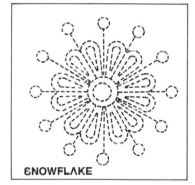

SNOWFLAKE

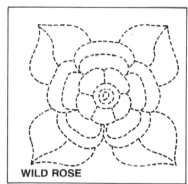

WILD ROSE

Quilting designs

Types of quilting designs/Borders

Border designs are made up of repeated patterns of motifs that frame and complement the main design on a quilt. To be effective, the border should relate to the overall character of the other quilt decorations. Traditionally, flowing motifs, such as undulating feathers and gracefully twined cables, were drawn. Now, almost any design suited to long and narrow spaces can be used; even simple geometric shapes and some all-over patterns are appropriate. Some designs are quite rigid in structure and require special planning (see opposite page). When a border turns corners, plan the design so that it flows smoothly around the corner, and is balanced on either side (see below).

Plan any border design on graph paper. Select the design and corner treatment, then work out from each corner to centres of sides, adjusting design repeats in between. In example above, tulip motif is placed in each corner and at centre of each side; graceful scroll design connects motifs.

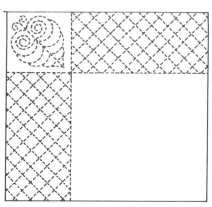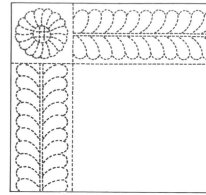

Corners can be filled with *unrelated motifs* provided border design is balanced on either side.

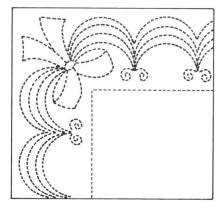

Or a *related motif can be introduced* at corners to bring the border to a conclusion.

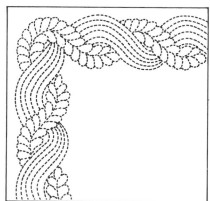

Or the *border design itself might be modified* to fit corners in one continuous line.

The patterns of rigidly structured designs develop basically from a square, and must be laid out according to the measurement of that square. For such a design to be successful, the border must be made long enough and wide enough to accommodate full repeats; partial repeats spoil the continuity. To be sure of full repeats, work out your border design on graph paper, then adjust quilt dimensions as needed. Because each border will consist entirely of full repeats, the corners will usually work out satisfactorily. When repeats have different motifs or internal patterns (see the top two designs on the far right), you will want particular motifs to fall at the corners and will have to plan for this.

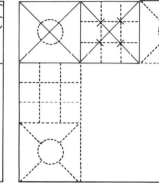

Design of concentric circles is like one on left, except overlaps are differently handled.

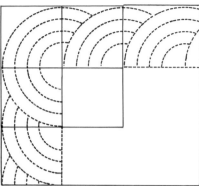

Alternating squares. Plan an *odd* number of squares placing crossed circle in corners.

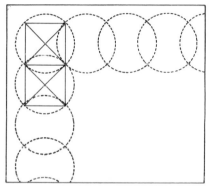

Wine-glass design stems from a circle drawn *around* basic square and made into template.

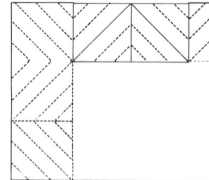

Squares of diagonals. Plan an *even* number of squares to have lines slanting towards centre.

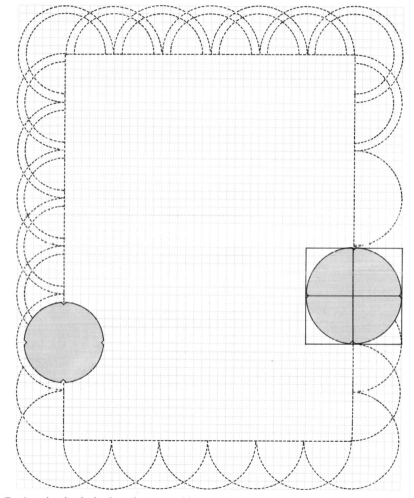

To plan a border design based on geometric repeats, divide the border into equal-size squares. The squares themselves may be the repeated shape (see top two designs, far right). In the design above, circles are developed from the square; templates are notched to show placing and intersecting points.

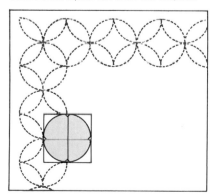

For petal-like motif, the template is made from a circle drawn *within* the square.

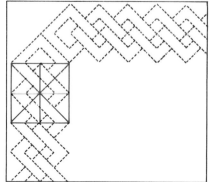

Interlocking links. Both their shape and placing evolve from a basic square as shown.

57

Quilting designs

Transferring and marking quilting designs

Quilt designs can be marked on fabric in a variety of ways. Which method you use will depend upon the type of design that is being marked and whether you will be marking it in or off the frame.

In-frame marking is done *after* the three quilting layers have been assembled and set into a frame or hoop. Designs must be marked a part at a time, as much as will fit within the exposed working area. In-frame markings are usually temporary, which allows the quilter to quilt each section after marking, thereby avoiding smudges and smears.

Off-frame methods (see far right and opposite page) are used more often. With these, the quilting design is marked on the top fabric layer *before* it is assembled with the other layers and set into a frame or hoop. Marking off the frame permits the entire design to be done at one time, a real advantage with highly complex designs.

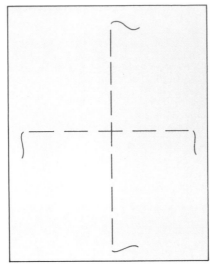

To prepare fabric for marking, press out any wrinkles or creases first. As a guide for proper placing of quilting designs, mark the centre of the piece by connecting side-to-side and top-to-bottom centre points with tacking threads.

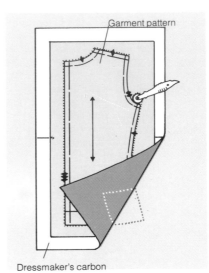
Garment pattern

Dressmaker's carbon

To mark odd shapes, such as parts of garments, lightly transfer the outline of each section on to the fabric, using dressmaker's carbon. Mark quilting design, but do not cut out garment sections until all quilting has been completed.

Off-frame methods

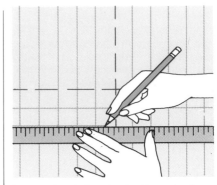

Straight-line designs begin with centring lines. *For a grid of squares,* use the tacked lines; space subsequent lines equally from these.

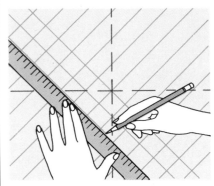

For a grid of diamonds, mark dividing lines from corner to corner; space the remaining lines evenly from these initial markings.

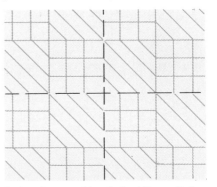

Design above combines both grid types. Notice the interesting pattern produced by having horizontal and vertical lines meet the diagonals.

In-frame methods

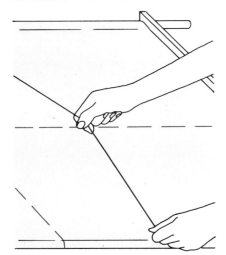

Chalking of straight-line designs such as squares, diagonals and channels is easily accomplished by snapping a taut chalk-coated string across a stretched quilt. Two people are needed to hold the ends of the string securely.

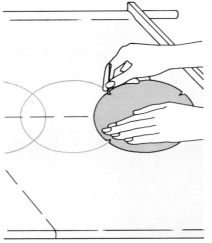

Needle marking, a useful though temporary method, usually follows a straight-edge or metre-stick, a template or a stencil. Holding needle like a pencil, draw it firmly across the fabric surface to produce an indentation of the design.

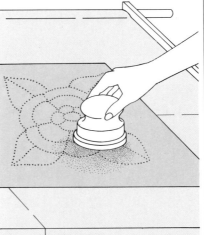

Perforated patterns are the usual choice for transferring intricate designs to top fabric. Make and use the perforated patterns as described for the off-frame method on the opposite page, but do not go over the dots with a pencil.

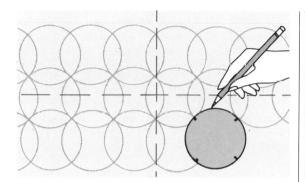

Templates are pattern shapes, usually cut from sturdy paper, that you simply trace around. Template for this design is notched on the edge to indicate where the shapes should overlap.

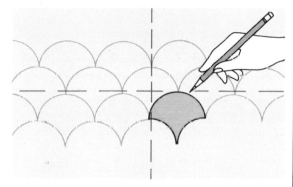

A frequent use of templates is repetition to produce an all over pattern, such as this shell design. When you are using a template for such all-over marking, work from the centre.

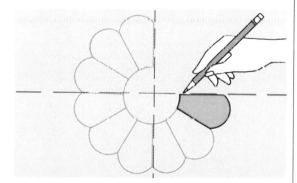

A template can also be the basis for forming a larger motif. The template used here is a wedge-shaped piece, called a *sector*, of a larger circle. Small centre circle is formed as well.

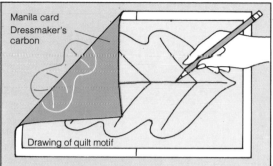

Manila card
Dressmaker's carbon

Drawing of quilt motif

To make your own stencil, work out a line design on paper, keeping the details within the motif very simple. Using dressmaker's carbon, transfer the design to sturdy paper or manila card.

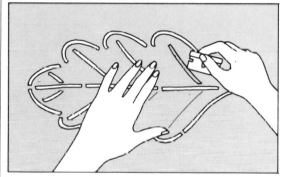

Cut out narrow channels along the drawn lines, using a single-edged razor blade or a craft knife. Be sure to leave connecting 'bridges' where lines intersect so that the stencil holds together.

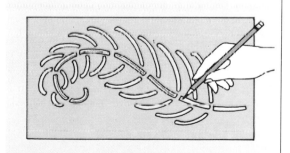

With stencil on fabric and fabric on firm surface, draw lines through slots with hard pencil, to mark simple quilting motifs. Do not use a soft pencil as the mark will be difficult to remove.

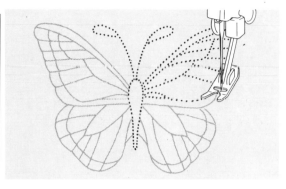

A perforated pattern is usually used to transfer intricate motifs. The design lines on the paper pattern may be pricked with a needle or stitched with an unthreaded sewing machine.

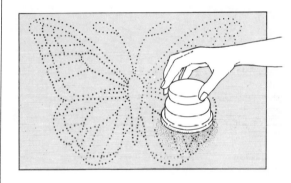

The perforated pattern is positioned on the fabric and a special powder called pounce is gently rubbed over the surface, leaving a dotted outline of the design on the fabric beneath.

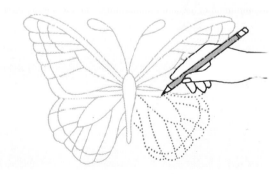

To reinforce the powder markings so that they do not disappear or smudge with handling, go over the dotted lines with a hard lead pencil or a dressmaker's chalk pencil.

Basic quilting techniques

Estimating quilt size and fabric amounts

To determine the size of a quilt, first consider the size of the bed the quilt is intended for. Measure the bed when it is fully made up, with sheet, blankets and pillows in place (see below). Use a flexible tape measure. Next, consider the way the quilt will be used; this will determine how much extra length is needed for the drop at the sides and at the foot of the bed, and whether or not a tuck-in allowance is desired for the pillows. For example, a quilt used as a bedspread will need a drop that falls to the floor and an extra allowance (about 38 cm) to tuck under the pillow. A short coverlet, on the other hand, need only hang down as far as the valance, and may

or may not be tucked in at the pillows. Many times, the depth of the drop is a matter of personal preference. If you are in doubt about what you prefer, drape a sheet over the bed, then fold and pin it in place until you arrive at a size of suitable and pleasing proportion. Remove the sheet and measure it. The overall size of a quilt is calculated from these basic measurements – bed length plus depth of drop, plus tuck-in allowance (if any), equals finished quilt length; bed width plus depth of drop (times 2) equals finished quilt width.

To estimate the fabric needed for a quilt, first determine its overall cutting size (see opposite page) and work out

your estimates according to that. Fabric requirements for a pieced top will depend, of course, on the patch design you select (see Patchwork). For a plain top, the amount of fabric required will depend upon the fabric width and its relation to the cutting size of the quilt width. For example, if the quilt width is narrower than the fabric width, only one length of fabric (a length equal to the quilt cutting length) is needed. If the quilt width is wider than one fabric width and anywhere up to twice as wide as the fabric width, two lengths of fabric are needed. You will need to add an extra amount to your estimate if you plan to use the same fabric as binding.

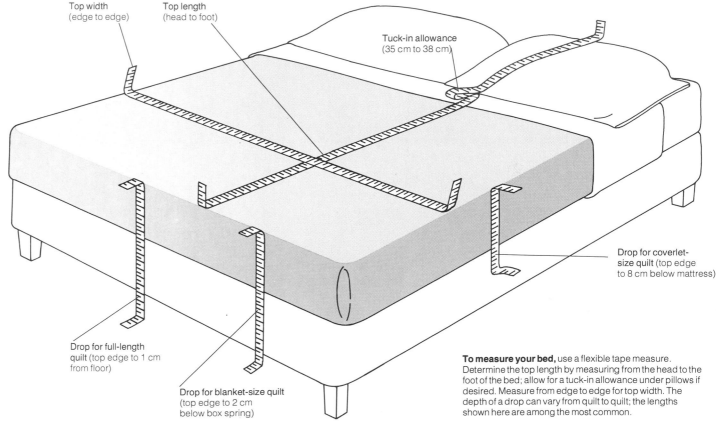

Top width
(edge to edge)

Top length
(head to foot)

Tuck-in allowance
(35 cm to 38 cm)

Drop for coverlet-
size quilt (top edge
to 8 cm below mattress)

Drop for full-length
quilt (top edge to 1 cm
from floor)

Drop for blanket-size quilt
(top edge to 2 cm
below box spring)

To measure your bed, use a flexible tape measure. Determine the top length by measuring from the head to the foot of the bed; allow for a tuck-in allowance under pillows if desired. Measure from edge to edge for top width. The depth of a drop can vary from quilt to quilt; the lengths shown here are among the most common.

Cutting quilt top and backing

To calculate cutting dimensions of quilt top and backing, consider these variables along with your estimated quilt size. Depending on the edge finish that you select, you may only need an additional 1 cm seam allowance all round, or you might have to add several centimetres to your calculations. To compensate for the 'shrinkage' that usually results from quilting, add a few more centimetres to your overall figures as well. A quilt can be as much as 8 cm to 16 cm smaller after quilting; as a rule, the thicker the wadding and heavier the quilting, the greater the reduction in size. When proper sizes are determined, cut out the top and backing. Mark the centre points on each side of both pieces to simplify alignment when they are assembled.

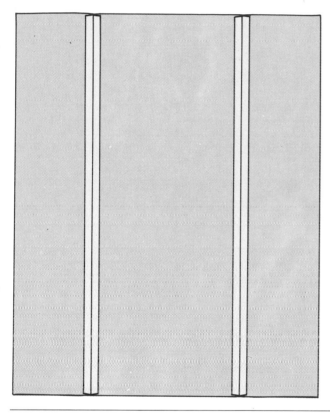

If the fabric is not wide enough for the top or backing, panels of appropriate widths can be joined to achieve the required measurement. When joining panels, avoid running a seam down the centre of the quilt; instead, use one central panel, usually a full fabric width, and add matching panels to each side. Press seams open. Any quilt top, whether patchwork, appliquéd or embroidered, can be enlarged in size if necessary by adding a border of the appropriate depth.

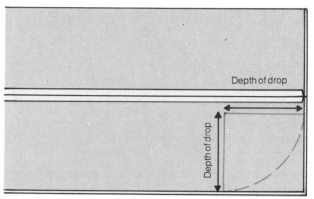

Rounding off corners for a quilted spread. On wrong side of quilt top, mark a square on corner of foot end; sides of square should equal depth of drop. Using a metrestick, measure from inner corner out, marking an arc as shown. Duplicate arc on opposite corner. Tack along arc to transfer curve to right side. Cut along arc after quilting has been completed.

Depth of drop

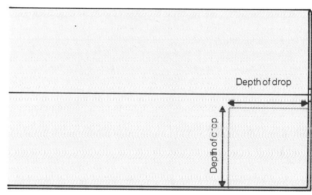

Cutting away corners to accommodate beds with foot posts. On right side of quilt top, mark a square on a corner of foot end; sides of square should equal depth of drop. Duplicate corner marking on opposite corner. Cut away corners along marked lines after quilting is completed.

Depth of drop

Cutting quilt filling

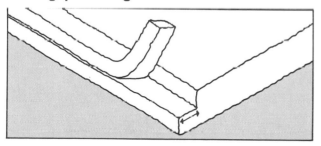

Cut wadding to same size as quilt top. If wadding must be pieced, separate it into two layers along one of the edges to be joined; cut a 1 cm strip from one layer. Separate and cut off a similar strip from the adjoining edge.

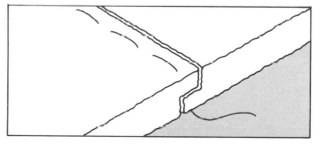

Overlap the cutaway edges as shown and tack the two together through both thicknesses. They are now joined with no tell-tale ridge.

Basic quilting techniques

Assembling quilt

When assembling any quilting project, stack the top, filling and backing carefully, then tack them together securely so they remain smooth and wrinkle-free throughout the quilting process. Proceed slowly when tacking; this can be the key to your quilting success. Even if you are using a frame or hoop, tacking is an important step, especially when working a large quilt; the stitches hold the layers together to prevent any shifting and bunching. For small projects, such as cushion covers, pin-tacking can be sufficient. If you are using the no-frame method (described lower right, on opposite page), or are quilting by machine (see p. 65), careful tacking is even more essential.

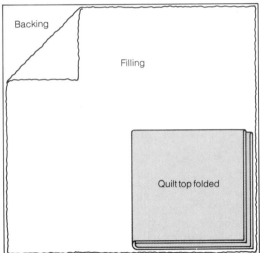

Backing

Filling

Quilt top folded

To assemble quilting layers, lay backing, wrong side up, on a hard, flat surface such as a table. Spread the wadding or other filling over the backing, then lay the top piece, right side up, over all.

For large quilts, lay backing on floor. Spread wadding over it, then stroke wadding with a metrestick to help remove any wrinkles. Do not stretch the wadding to fit, as it may tear. Fold quilt top into quarters with right side folded inside, and place it on one corner of the filling as shown; use the marked centre points on backing and top piece for accurate alignment. Carefully unfold the top, and again use the metrestick to smooth it in place. Do not kneel or stand on the fabric to reach the centre; this can cause hidden wrinkles in the filling and the backing.

Tack the three layers together in a sunburst pattern to avoid forming a lump of filling in the centre. Using large running stitches, start from the centre and work out towards the edges. Tack only from the top, being careful not to shift layers. As a general rule, there should be a tacked line about every 15 cm around the edges; tack more generously if the quilting will be done off a frame or hoop. Tacking stitches may be cut and released as needed during the quilting process.

Setting quilt into frame

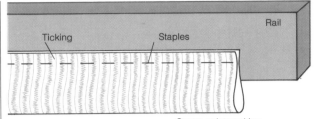

Ticking   Staples   Rail

Centre point marking

Staple ticking or other sturdy fabric to the rails as shown on p. 51. Mark the centre points of each rail for proper alignment when attaching the quilting project.

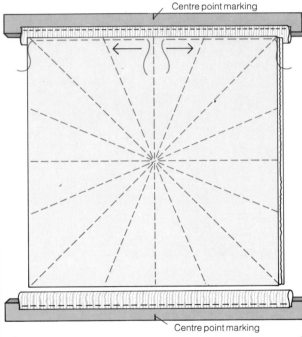

Centre point marking

To attach quilt to rails, lay the tacked quilt on the floor and position the rails at each end, matching the centre points of rails and quilt top. Tack the quilt to the ticking along each rail, working from centre point out to each side.

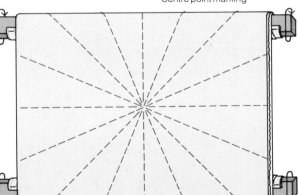

Roll the quilt evenly and tightly on to each rail so a central area is exposed for quilting.

Attach the rails to the stretchers, adjusting them both so the quilt is held taut and straight, without sagging. Check for any wrinkles on the top and the backing of the exposed working area.

Secure the sides of the quilt by pinning cotton tape to the edges, and looping it around the stretchers as shown; pin at about 8 cm intervals. After completing the quilting within the exposed area, reveal a fresh section by unpinning the taped sides and rolling the completed part on to one of the rails. Secure the sides again as before.

Setting quilt into hoop

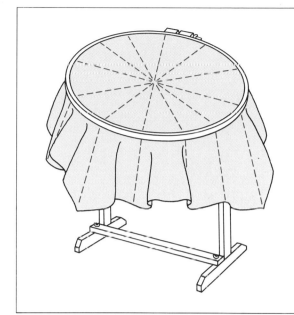

To set quilt or any other project into a hoop, place the centre of the tacked project over the inner hoop. Work out any fullness from the quilt by smoothing it over the edges of the hoop. Slide the outer ring in place and tighten the adjustment screw to keep the layers taut.

After quilting within this central area, remove the hoop and re-position the quilt to expose a fresh section; work from this central area out towards the edges. To quilt up to the edges, use a smaller hoop along the sides, or quilt without a hoop.

No-frame method

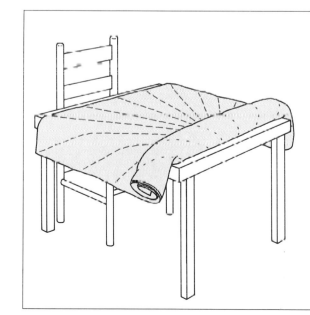

To quilt without a frame or hoop, place the tacked project over a table or ironing board so that its weight is fully supported. Do not allow large portions of the project to hang heavily over the sides of the table; this can cause pulling and some distortion. If necessary, roll or fold up the sides so they are properly supported. For small projects, you can simply spread the work over your lap.

Basic quilting techniques

Basic hand-quilting techniques

To quilt by hand, use an even *running stitch* that is short and closely spaced so as to give the illusion of an unbroken line (see below). Though a matching thread is the usual choice, a white thread or one which contrasts with the fabric can be used if you prefer. To avoid excessive tangling, use a single length of thread, no more than 50 cm long. Ideally, the quilting stitches should be fine (about 2 mm long), and even on both the top and backing. As you become more proficient with experience, you can increase your working speed by picking up several stitches on the needle before pushing it through; you will begin to develop a rhythm as your needle rocks back and forth, picking up the stitches. To facilitate this rhythmic motion, keep your quilting project slightly less than drum-tight when working in a frame or hoop.

You will also find stitching easier and more natural if you start an arm's length away, and quilt towards yourself, changing your position as the quilting dictates. Extra-thick fillings should be avoided, especially if you are working an intricate design.

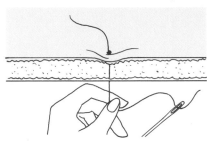
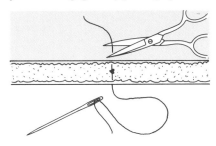

To start a line of quilting, knot end of thread and insert needle from the top through all three layers. Gently but firmly pull the thread from underneath so knot slips through the top layer and lodges in the filling. Cut off any thread end that may be visible on the surface.

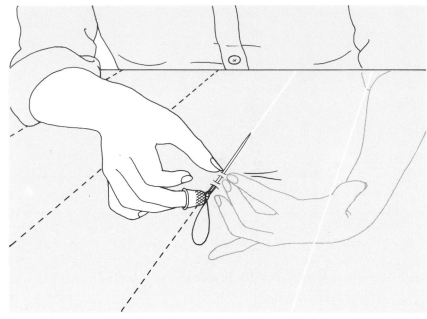

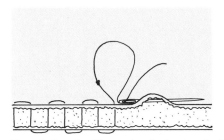
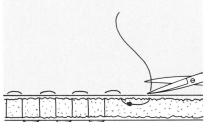

To end a line of quilting, make a knot on top of quilting surface. Insert needle a stitch length away and run needle through filling for a short distance; bring needle up, and gently pull the thread so knot slips through the top layer. Cut off thread end close to the surface.

To quilt with running stitch, grasp needle with thumb and forefinger; take a few stitches, and push needle through with middle finger. To be sure needle penetrates all layers, hold other hand beneath the surface so tip of finger actually feels point each time a stitch is taken.

Hand-quilting tips

For curved or circular motifs, use a double length of thread and start quilting at the 2 o'clock position; quilt in each direction from this starting point so that you are able to quilt towards yourself at all times.

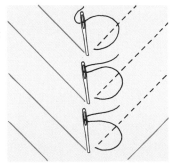

Keep several threaded needles in action. Quilt on a design line until it turns away from you or until you reach the end of an exposed quilting area. Leave needles on top layer and pick them up after you have shifted your position or have rolled a fresh area on to the frame.

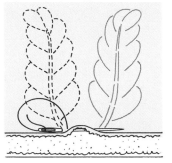

Avoid unnecessary starts and stops when quilting closely spaced motifs. Instead of knotting each time, simply run the needle from a completed motif through the filling and start again at next motif.

Machine quilting

Quilting with a sewing machine creates a durable and even stitching line that takes a fraction of the hand-quilting time. While it is possible to quilt almost any kind of project by machine, it is not always convenient to do so. Machine quilting is especially appropriate for small projects, such as cot quilts, garment sections and household articles, because they are easy to manoeuvre under the needle and can be made to fit under the arm of the machine when necessary. (It is also best for hard-to-quilt fabrics.) For such large projects as full-sized quilts and bedspreads, the sewing area must be modified and the sequence of quilting precisely planned to allow for the bulk as it passes through the sewing machine (see above right). If possible, avoid a single large piece by dividing the project into smaller sections – bedspread panels, for example, or quilt blocks. These can be quilted separately and joined later (see unit method of quilting on p. 69).

The sewing machine also limits the type of quilting design that is advisable. Avoid elaborate or curved designs that require cumbersome and frequent turning under the machine needle; they are both awkward and time-consuming. Simple quilting designs composed of straight lines are better choices and can be worked quickly and easily, especially if the lines of quilting extend from one edge of the project to the other. For this reason, all-over grid designs are highly suitable and frequently chosen (see lower right corner).

When preparing a project for machine quilting, be sure to tack generously so the layers do not shift as they are being fed through the machine. To avoid unsightly puckers, adjust the machine by loosening the tension and decreasing the pressure. Set the stitch length to medium-size stitches and test the setting on a complete sample of top, filling and backing tacked together.

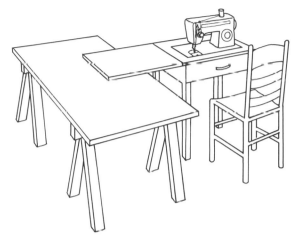

To modify the sewing area for large projects, move the sewing machine out into an open space. Raise a large piece of cardboard or wood on trestles or chairs to the level of the sewing machine and place alongside the machine. This extension will support a large, heavy project, and so make it easier to manoeuvre.

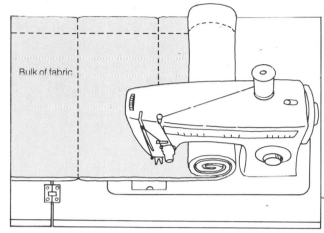

When quilting by machine, be sure to plan the direction and sequence of your stitching so that the bulk of the project always lies to the left of the needle. When working on a large project, such as a quilt, extend the working area as shown on left; roll the project up tightly enough to fit under the sewing machine arm as it becomes necessary.

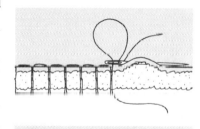

To secure thread ends that start or end away from raw edges, leave long thread ends on both top and bottom of quilted surface. Thread one of the ends through a needle and run needle through filling for a short distance.

Bring needle out, and cut off excess thread end close to the quilting surface. Run the other thread end through the filling in the same way.

If quilting line starts or ends at the edges, the thread ends need not be secured; the final edge finish (such as a binding) will keep the stitches from pulling out.

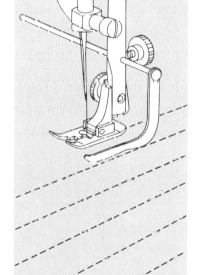

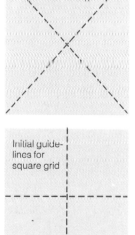

Initial guidelines for diamond grid

Initial guidelines for square grid

Use a quilting guide-bar attachment to quilt grid designs. Its adjustable bar extends out from the machine foot and falls along a guideline so that each quilting line can be equally spaced. Stitch initial guidelines as shown in the small drawings, then use the attachment to quilt lines on either side.

Other quilting techniques

Tying a quilt
Stuffed quilting
Corded quilting
Quilting in units
Sectional quilting
Pillow quilting
Puff quilting

Tying a quilt

Tying is a method of holding a quilt together without making lines of running stitches. To tie a quilt, take a single stitch at regular intervals through all layers, leaving thread ends long enough to tie in a knot on the quilt top. Tying is faster than quilting with a running stitch, and more practical when the filling is thick or otherwise difficult to handle. Also, crazy quilts, which have no filling, are usually tied. This technique is not suitable when the filling may shift with washing, and so needs the control of stitching. For tying, you will need a large-eyed crewel needle and a strong decorative thread, such as stranded cotton, pearl cotton, narrow ribbon or knitting yarn.

This quilt top is secured to the wadding and backing with knots tied at regular intervals.

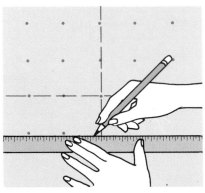

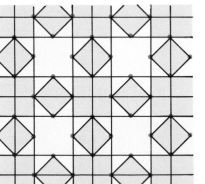

To prepare a quilt top for tying, mark its horizontal and vertical centres with tacking lines. Then, moving out from them with a ruler and a pencil or chalk, indicate the points for tying. Make sure the points are equally spaced and no more than 10 cm to 15 cm apart.

On a patchwork top, you can follow the design of the quilt to place the points for tying. Keep spacing as even as possible, and try not to leave large areas untied.

After marking, tack the top, filling and backing together as shown on p. 62.

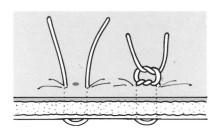

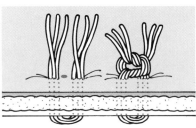

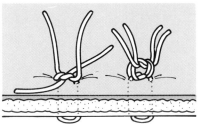

Make a tie at each of the marks on the top layer as follows. Take a stitch down through all three layers, then come up, leaving enough thread at ends to tie a reef knot, as shown. Trim ends to a uniform length, usually about 2 cm.

To make tufts, thread a needle with two or three lengths of thread. Take a stitch as above, and tie all of the ends in a reef knot. Trim ends evenly.

Another way of tufting, useful when a quilt is difficult to penetrate with multiple strands of thread, is to make the stitch with one length of thread and then add one or more lengths while tying the reef knot, as illustrated.

Stuffed quilting

Stuffed quilting is a type of quilting in which only certain sections of the stitch design are padded, bringing them into relief and giving dimension to the design. It is especially effective on a solid-colour fabric. To do this kind of quilting, you stitch the design through two layers of fabric (top and backing) and then insert the filling (synthetic or cotton wadding) between them by means of slits cut in the backing. The top layer is usually a tightly woven fabric, such as cotton or poplin. Because the filling is inserted through the backing, the best choice for this is a loosely woven fabric, such as lightweight muslin, voile or cheesecloth. To protect the back of the quilt and conceal the ragged edges left

from the insertion of filling, the work should be lined with fabric of a type similar to that used for the top layer. For quilting stitches, use cotton quilting thread or a synthetic thread of a similar weight. Silk twist can be substituted for a richer look.

The designs best suited to this type of quilting include motifs and geometric shapes composed of many small sections, as shown in the photograph (right). It is difficult to stuff large areas uniformly. If you want to try a quick, modern approach to stuffed quilting, find a printed fabric with a distinct motif composed of small, enclosed areas, and use the techniques described below to put the motifs in relief.

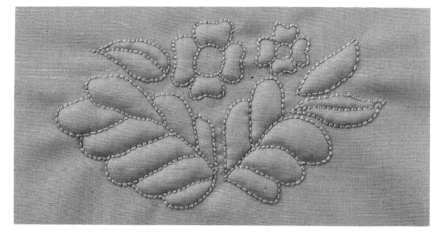

Leaves and flower petals above are stuffed with small pieces of wadding inserted through backing.

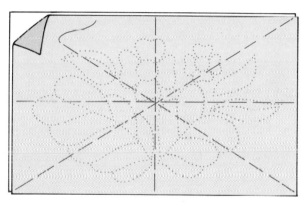

1. Transfer the quilt design to the fabric, using pounce, pricking or other invisible method. Then, with raw edges and grainlines aligned, tack fabric to backing through horizontal and vertical centres, and diagonally from corner to corner, as shown.

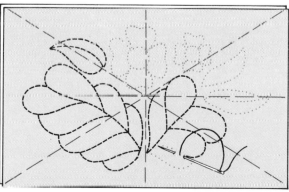

2. Hand-sew the fabric layers together along the design lines, using either a backstitch or an even running stitch. Or straight-stitch around the design by machine. Keep stitches as small as fabric thicknesses will permit. If you prefer a stronger marking line, transfer the design to the backing fabric, tracing the mirror image of the design. When stitching is complete, remove tacking.

3. Cut a slit in centre of one small section of the muslin backing. Make the slit slightly off grain to avoid weakening the fabric. Stuff the section lightly with filling so the area is raised but not so packed as to distort the fabric.

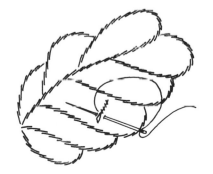

4. Close the slit with oversewing, as shown. Repeat the procedure of cutting a centre slit, stuffing the section and closing the slit for each of the design areas that you want to pad.

Other quilting techniques

Corded quilting

Italian or corded quilting is a type of quilting in which linear designs are raised from the background with a cord or wool filling. This kind of quilting is often combined with stuffed quilting to accentuate both the lines and shapes of the design. There are two ways to achieve the raised look. The first and most common method is to stitch the quilt design, in parallel lines, through two layers of fabric. The resulting channels are then threaded with wool or other rope-like filling. Pre-shrink the filling to avoid puckering after laundering. The top fabric should be tightly woven, the back fabric a loose weave.

Use cotton or synthetic quilting thread or, for a richer look, stitch with silk twist. The piece must be lined to protect and conceal the filling insertions.

The second method involves only one layer of fabric. The cord is laid under the fabric and stitched in place at the same time. Since only one layer of fabric is used, this method is suitable for projects where a backing or lining is undesirable. For either method, use a soft cotton cord or wool to fill the channels. Select the thickness according to the width between the parallel lines; the cord should fill the space so the channel is raised, but not so tightly that it distorts the fabric.

METHOD I

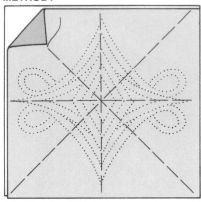

1. Transfer the quilt design to the fabric, using pounce, pricking or other invisible method. Then, with raw edges and grainlines aligned, tack fabric to backing through horizontal and vertical centres, and diagonally from corner to corner, as shown.

2. Sew the two fabric layers together along marked lines, using a small running stitch or backstitch, or the straight stitch on your machine. Keep stitches small and even.

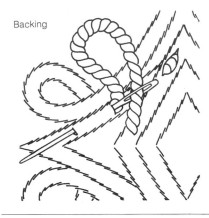

Backing

3. On the backing side, make a small slit in one of the channels formed by the parallel stitching. Using a blunt needle or bodkin, insert the wool or cord filling a bit at a time. Run the needle through the channel for about 2 cm and bring the needle out, pulling the cord taut; insert the needle in the same exit hole and repeat, taking care not to pierce the top fabric.

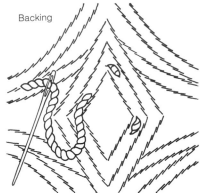

Backing

4. When filling a curve or corner, proceed as in Step 3, but do not pull the cord taut. Instead, leave a bit of slack at the turn to fill in the space, as shown. This will prevent puckering at these points on the top of the quilt.

METHOD II

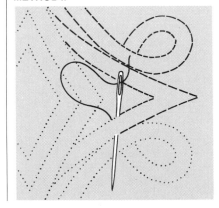

1. Transfer the quilt design to the right side of the fabric. Insert the fabric in a frame or hoop to leave both hands free for working. Use a sharp needle and buttonhole twist. Holding the cord in position underneath the fabric with one hand, backstitch along the parallel lines, alternating stitches from side to side.

2. The crossed threads on the underside of the fabric hold the cord within the design lines and keep it flat against the fabric. As you work, keep the stitches even and the tension consistent.

Quilting in units/Sectional quilting

Quilting in units simplifies the making of large quilts or other quilted items by dividing the work into small, manageable units. **Sectional quilting** enables you to quilt one block or panel at a time. This technique, adapted from traditional quilting, is especially appropriate when you want a portable project or when you want to stitch by machine. **Pillow quilting** and **puff patchwork** (described on the next page) are contemporary techniques that also enable you to stitch and stuff one block at a time before assembling several of them.

Although these methods are generally limited to simple quilting designs and simple patchwork, they do offer several advantages: they require little work space, they need no frame or hoop, and all or part of the stitching involved can be done by machine, which makes the work considerably faster.

Sectional quilting, or dividing a quilt into sections for quilting, makes it easier to handle. Although adaptable to any size project, this technique is particularly helpful when it would be awkward to quilt a big project by machine. No mat-

ter how large the finished quilt is to be, it can be divided for quilting purposes into sections no bigger than one of its blocks.

To divide a project into sections, use the existing seams in the item. For example, a patchwork or appliqué quilt top can be quilted so that each block constitutes a section, or the quilt can be divided into groups of blocks. A border for such a quilt would be another separate section for quilting. These parts would be joined together after the quilting of all of the parts is completed.

This seaming approach can also be used for quilting and assembling a garment. For example, the fronts and back of a waistcoat can be quilted separately and then stitched together at the side seams. When choosing fabric for backing, remember that in this technique of sectional quilting, the backing fabric functions as a kind of lining because all of the raw edges are enclosed. No extra lining need be added for a finished look.

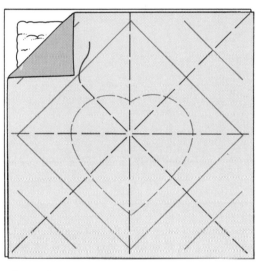

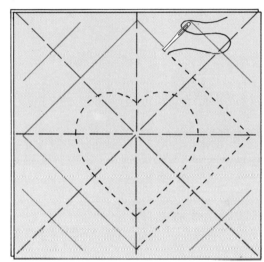

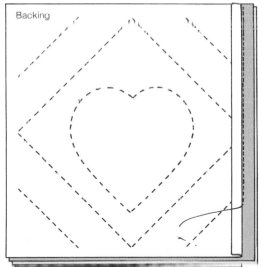

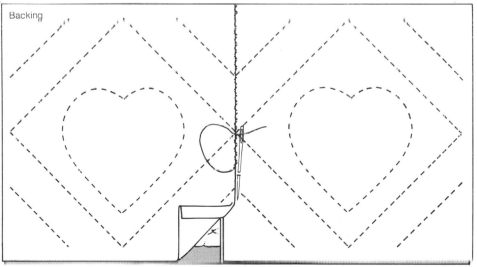

1. Cut the top and backing the same size for each section, allowing a 5 mm seam allowance on each side. Cut the filling for each section to the same size, but omit the seam allowances. Transfer the quilting design to the top fabric. Stack the layers and tack them together through the centre, as shown.

2. Quilt the section, being careful to start and stop the quilting 1.5 cm from the seamline so the seam allowances are left free for joining and turning back. Remove the tacking

3. To assemble, place adjoining sections together, right sides facing, and join the *top fabrics only*, stitching the seam by hand or machine.

4. To finish the back, place the sections face down on a flat surface. Finger-press the seam open. The filling edges should meet; if they overlap, trim off excess. Turn under the seam allowance of one edge of the backing and slipstitch it securely to the backing of the adjoining section. Where necessary, go back and finish the quilting to the seamline.

Other quilting techniques

Quilting in units/Pillow quilting

In pillow quilting, each patchwork piece is backed, filled and finished on all sides before the pieces are assembled. The effect of the finished quilt is similar to outline quilting in that the shape of each individually stuffed piece stands out. Any patchwork block or one-patch design that is a straight-edged geometric shape can be used. If the backing and top fabric are the same, the quilt will be identical on both sides; to create a reversible quilt, use a contrasting fabric for the backing. Or you could use up remnants by cutting each patch from a different fabric. For stuffing, use synthetic wadding.

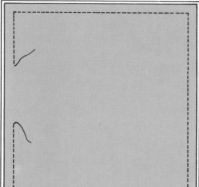

Pillows are sewn and stuffed before assembly.

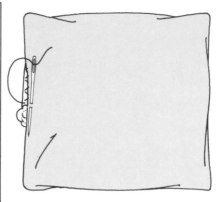

Cut a patch and a backing from the same template. Align them, right sides facing; stitch around edge, leaving an opening for turning.

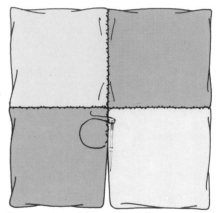

Carefully turn patch right side out. Add filling through the opening, stuffing lightly and evenly. Slipstitch the opening closed by hand.

To assemble the finished patches, butt the edges and join them by hand with a slipstitch, or by machine with a fine zigzag stitch.

Quilting in units/Puff quilting

In puff quilting, a top patch is eased or tucked to fit a smaller backing so the top patch can be heavily stuffed to produce a puffy look. The edges are concealed after assembly with a lining, so the backing can be muslin. For stuffing, use synthetic wadding. Because of its puffiness, this style is confined to quilts and cushion covers. Although any one-patch design can be used, straight-sided shapes are easiest to work with. Two templates are needed: one for the patch, and another, which is the same basic shape but smaller, for the backing. The patch is usually one and a half times larger than the backing – for example, a 15 cm top fabric will be eased to fit a 10 cm backing. The greater the difference between the sizes, the puffier the finished unit will be.

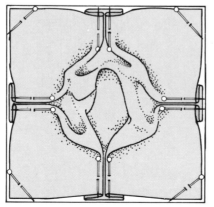

Pieces in puff quilting are more heavily stuffed.

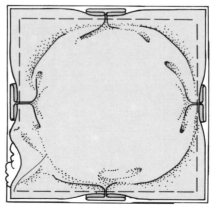

Wrong sides facing, pin patch to backing at corners. Match centre points at sides and pin. Fold excess fabric in centre into tucks as shown.

Tack around the edge by hand or machine, leaving an opening to one side of one tuck. Add filling, then tack the opening closed by hand.

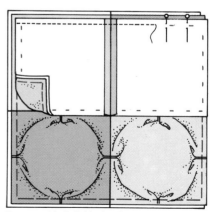

To assemble individual units, sew seams with right sides facing. To finish, line the entire piece or add a backing (for directions see p. 74):

Finishing edges

Self-finished edges
Extended binding
Slipstitched edges
Bound edges
Applying binding
Handling corners
Lining and interlining

Self-finished edges/Extended binding

When the quilting part of a project is completed, it is still necessary to finish the edges. Several methods are available; the choice depends upon the type of quilt you are making and its design. The first, called the self-finished edge, utilises only the quilt top and backing.

There are two kinds of self-finish: the **extended binding**, which can be used only if the backing fabric is of the same quality as the top fabric; and the **slip-stitched edge** (explained on the next page). To make an extended binding, you must plan it before you cut the main pieces; in order for the extra fabric to be folded up over the raw edges on to the quilt top, the backing must be cut larger than the top. This method can also be worked in reverse—that is, the top fabric can be cut larger and folded down over the backing.

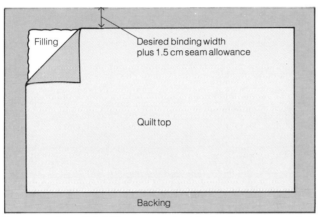

To prepare for self-finishing, you must cut the backing large enough to extend beyond the top piece by the desired binding width plus a 1.5 cm seam allowance on all four sides. Cut both top and filling to finished quilt size.

After quilting, press up the seam allowances of the backing. Then fold it over the edge to form the binding and slipstitch it to top fabric. Decide before you begin to stitch which corner treatment (below) you want to use.

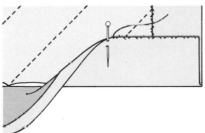
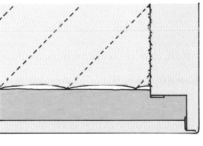

For a straight corner, slipstitch one side of the quilt. To reduce the bulk, trim away some of the corner fabric as shown.

Turn up the adjacent side and slipstitch it to the binding, then to the top fabric, as shown.

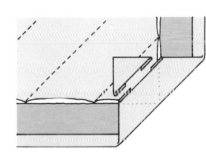
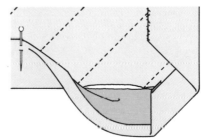

For a mitred corner, fold up the corner of the backing fabric so the diagonal fold lies at the corner point of the top fabric. Trim off the corner of the backing as shown.

Fold up one side of the binding and slipstitch it in place. Then fold up the adjacent side and slipstitch it in place. Slipstitch the mitre – the diagonal line where the two edges of the binding meet – to close it.

Finishing edges

Self-finished edges/Slipstitched edges

The slipstitched method of finishing a quilt creates an inconspicuous finished edge, formed simply by folding under the seam allowances for both the top and backing fabrics, and slipstitching the folds together. This method requires no additional fabric, but trimmings, such as piping, ricrac, or ruffles, can be inserted between the folds if desired. When using the slipstitched method, be sure the quilting stitches stop about 1 cm from the edge so the seam allowances can be folded under. Do not stop the quilting too far from the edges, however, because this method does not secure the filling along the edges.

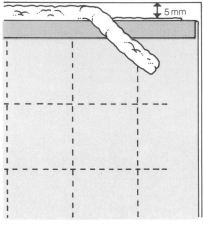

Line up the edges of the quilt top and backing. Trim the wadding so it is about 5 mm shorter than the top and backing fabrics.

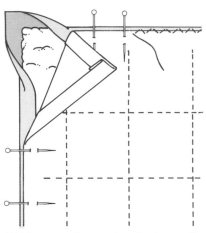

Fold the seam allowance from the top over the filling. Turn under the backing seam allowance. Align folds; pin, then slipstitch them together.

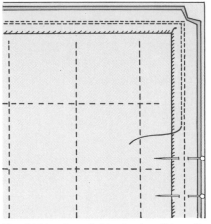

To add trimming, pin trimming to quilt top with raw edges of both trimming and quilt facing in the same direction; stitch along the quilt seamline.

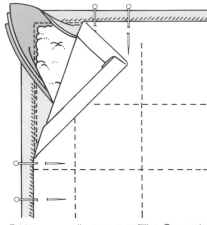

Fold top seam allowance over filling. Turn under backing seam allowance. Pin. Slipstitch backing to trimming along stitched line of trimming.

Bound edges

Binding is a type of edge finish that calls for a separate strip of fabric to cover the raw edges of the quilt. It is neat, durable, and especially practical if the raw edges are worn or uneven from having been stretched in the quilting frame. Binding is also recommended for finishing a quilted garment in order to avoid a bulky hem. This edge finish should be planned from the beginning so you can buy enough fabric. Finished bindings are traditionally narrow, about 5 mm to 1 cm wide. Cut from a contrasting fabric, binding becomes an attractive trimming. Binding can be cut either from the straight grain or on the bias of the fabric. Curved edges require bias binding; either will do for straight and angular edges. There are both single and double bindings. Single is used most often for quilts; for greater durability, however, you can use a double binding.

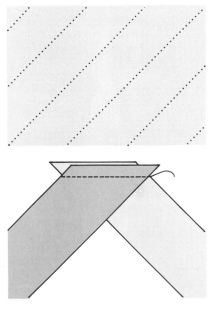

To make bias bindings, cut strips of fabric along the true bias of the fabric. For single binding, cut strips four times the desired finished width. For double binding, cut strips six times the desired finished width.

To join bias strips, place two together as shown and stitch on the straight grain of the fabric. Press the seam open.

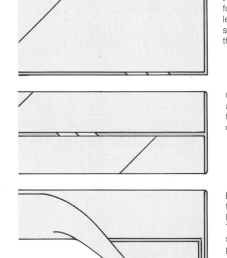

For a single binding, fold the strip in half lengthwise with wrong sides facing and press the fold lightly.

Open the pressed strip and fold the edges in so that they meet at the centre; press.

For a double binding, fold the strip in half lengthwise and press. Then fold this halved strip in thirds and press.

Applying binding

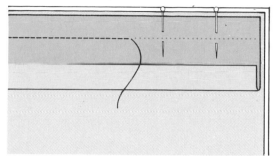

To apply single binding, open one folded edge. With right side of binding facing quilt top, pin binding to the edge of the quilt. Stitch along the foldline of the binding.

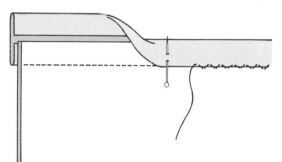

Press binding up. Turn it over raw edge so fold meets stitched line on the backing. Pin it in place and slipstitch to seamline by hand.

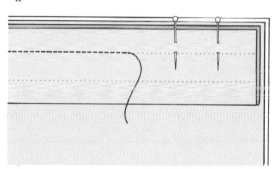

To apply double binding, open both folds. Pin binding to the quilt top with raw edges of binding and quilt aligned. Stitch binding to quilt along foldline nearest the edge.

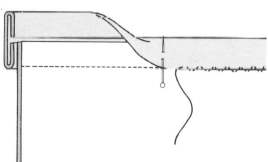

Press binding up, turning in second fold. Turn it over the raw edge so fold meets stitched line on backing. Pin it in place and slipstitch to seamline by hand.

Handling corners

Bound corners, whether curved or straight, are handled in different ways. If a corner is curved, binding can be eased to fit around it. To do this, binding must be bias. If a corner is square, the binding can be applied so that corners are straight, as below, or mitred (see next page). The techniques for all three remain the same whether the binding is single or double.

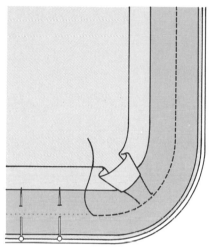

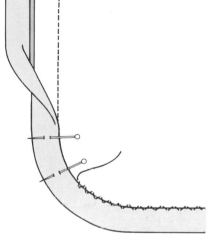

To bind a curved corner, pin bias binding to quilt edge as shown. Gently stretch the binding as you round the corner. Stitch along fold.

Press binding up and fold over to the backing. Binding will mould naturally over curved raw edge of quilt. Slipstitch to backing at stitch line.

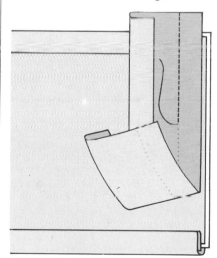

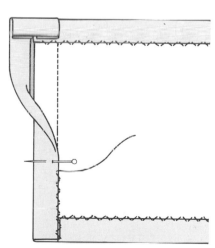

For straight corners, bind two opposite sides of the quilt. Then pin and stitch binding to one of the two remaining sides, letting the binding extend 1 cm at both ends.

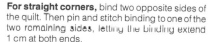

Turn the extended portion of the binding over the bound edge, then finish binding the raw edge in the usual way. Repeat the same procedure to bind the remaining raw edge.

Finishing edges

Handling corners/Mitring

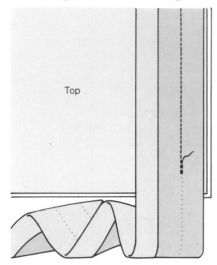

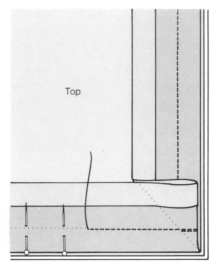

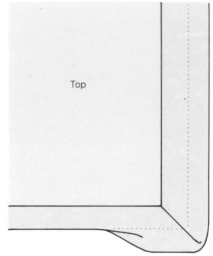

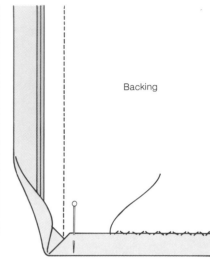

For a mitred corner, pin binding to one raw edge of quilt. Stitch along binding fold nearest raw edge, stopping and securing stitches at point where adjacent seam will cross this seamline.

Fold free binding to right, perpendicular to stitched edge, forming diagonal fold. Place binding parallel with lower edge and align right-hand fold with right edge. Stitch as shown.

Press the binding away from the quilt top, then fold it over raw edge to backing. A mitre will form on the quilt top. Another mitre will be formed by manipulating binding on back.

On backing side, bring folded edge to stitched line; pin. Fold excess binding under at corner, then bring adjacent binding together to form a mitre. Slipstitch binding along fold, and mitre.

Lining and interlining

Some quilting methods, the raised quilting techniques and puff patchwork in particular, require a lining or interlining to protect the stitching on the backing and to hide any raw edges. A lining is appropriate if you want to finish an item – such as a quilt, place-mat or tablecloth – to the edge. You will also want to use an interlining if you are working on a project, such as a garment, where the quilting will be seamed to adjoining sections, or where you want to finish the edge with a binding. A lining or interlining should be planned from the beginning so you can allow for the extra fabric that is needed.

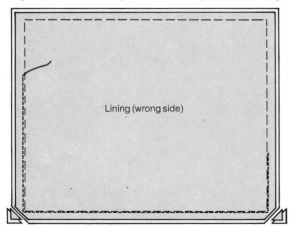

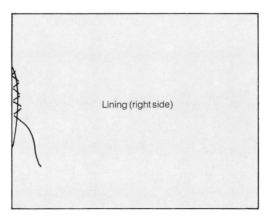

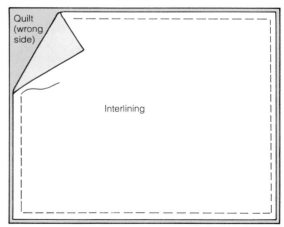

To line a quilt to the edge, cut the lining the same size as the quilt. Pin or tack the lining to the quilt with right sides facing. Stitch around the edge, leaving an opening for turning.

Remove the pins or tacking stitches. Trim off the corners to reduce bulk and turn the quilt right side out. Turn under the seam allowances of the opening and slipstitch it closed.

To interline. Cut interlining the same size as quilt. With wrong sides facing, tack interlining to quilt along edges. Treat quilt and interlining as one layer during subsequent construction.

Care of quilts

Washing, drying,
pressing and storing
Repairing damage

Careful laundering, proper storage and attention to repairs will prolong the life of quilts and quilted items.

To wash a quilt by machine, use a mild detergent and gentle agitation. Avoid bleach, harsh detergents or too much detergent, because these chemicals weaken textile fibres. Do not spin a quilt dry; this strains the quilting stitches and may break them. When washing by hand, use mild soap and do not twist or wring the quilt. Roll it in towels to remove as much moisture as possible.

To dry a quilt, tumble in a dryer or hang it on a clothes-line. Or, if you have the space, dry the quilt by spreading it out flat on a clean sheet.

If a quilt is made from fabrics such as wool, silk or velvet, which must be dry-cleaned, have this done as seldom as possible. Dry-cleaning chemicals wear out textile fabrics in time.

To press a quilt, pad the ironing board with a thick towel. Place the item quilted side down and steam-press lightly. Never press with the weight of the iron on the quilt.

Because textiles need to breathe, store a quilt by rolling it in a clean bed sheet. Do not use plastic because it prevents the air from circulating. Air a stored quilt at least once a year by hanging it on a clothes-line, preferably on a breezy day, and launder it approximately every five years to prevent the fabric from yellowing. If a quilt is folded for storage in a chest, re-fold it yearly to avoid permanent creases.

Quilts can easily be repaired if damaged. Re-binding will renew a worn edge. Remove the original binding before applying the new one. To blend new with faded colours, prepare the new binding fabric by washing it repeatedly or by bleaching it in the sun. To mend broken quilting stitches, insert the damaged area in a small hoop, carefully pull out the broken threads and re-stitch.

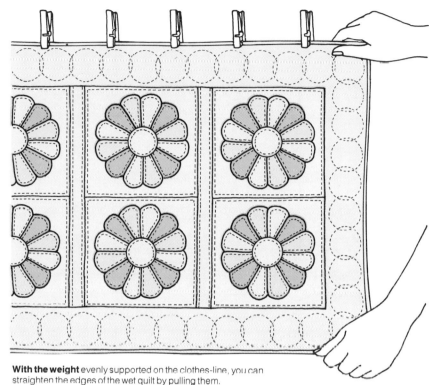

With the weight evenly supported on the clothes-line, you can straighten the edges of the wet quilt by pulling them.

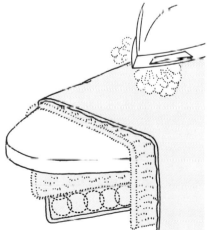

To press a quilt, steam-press lightly with the item quilted side down on a thick towel.

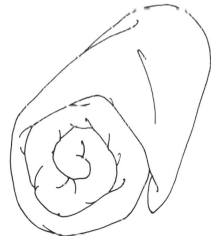

Store a quilt by rolling it up in a clean sheet. Do not use plastic.

Index

Suppliers

J.E. Beale Plc
26/36 Silver Street
Bedford
MK40 1PE
Telephone: 01234 353292
(needlework materials)

Harrods Ltd
Knightsbridge
London SW1
Telephone: 0171 730 1234
(needlework materials)

John Lewis
Oxford Street
London W1
Telephone: 0171 629 7711
(needlework materials)

Mace & Nairn
89 Crane Street
Salisbury
Wilts
Telephone: 01722 336903
(embroidery materials)

Christine Riley's Embroidery Shop
53 Barclay Street
Stonehaven
Kincardineshire
AB3 2AR
Telephone: 01569 763238
(needlework materials)

Royal School of Needlework
Apartment 12A
Hampton Court Palace
East Molesey
Surrey
KT8 9AU
Telephone: 0181 943 1432
(needlework materials)

Specialist Crafts Ltd
PO Box 247
Leicester
LE1 9QS
Telephone: 01533 510405
(craft and needlework supplies)

Spinning Jenny
Market Place
Masham
Ripon
N. Yorks
Telephone: 01765 689351
(embroidery, appliqué and patchwork materials)

Photographic credits
page 22 Rose design quilt, The Gazebo.
page 47 Baby Blocks quilt, The Gazebo.
page 48 Grandmother's Flower Garden quilt. Thos. K. Woodward.

Also available in this series:

Reader's Digest Needlecraft Guide
CANVAS WORK

Whatever your level of experience, you'll find all the practical information you need to stitch your own glorious designs in this one handy volume.

- More than 450 illustrations and photographs
- Step-by-step diagrams for every stitch and technique
- Over 75 stitches, from basic tent stitch to intricate rococo

Reader's Digest Needlecraft Guide
CROCHET & LACEMAKING

All the practical information you need for these crafts is at your fingertips, from useful and encouraging advice on crochet to the secrets of the lacemaker's art, including needlepoint, filet, woven and bobbin methods.

- More than 400 illustrations and photographs
- Detailed explanation on following patterns
- An essential reference guide

Reader's Digest Needlecraft Guide
EMBROIDERY

Open this book and find all the practical information you need to take up your needle and begin stitching with confidence.

- More than 700 illustrations and photographs
- Over 75 stitches fully explained, from the simple to the complex
- A wide range of techniques illustrated with step-by-step sequences